THE

WAIT

DEVOTIONAL

DAILY INSPIRATIONS FOR
FINDING THE LOVE OF YOUR LIFE
AND THE LIFE YOU LOVE

DeVON FRANKLIN
AND MEAGAN GOOD

HOWARD BOOKS
AN IMPRINT OF SIMON & SCHUSTER, INC.

New York   London   Toronto   Sydney   New Delhi

Howard Books
An Imprint of Simon & Schuster, Inc.
1230 Avenue of the Americas
New York, NY 10020

First Howard Books hardcover edition October 2017

HOWARD and colophon are trademarks of Simon & Schuster, Inc.

For information about special discounts for bulk purchases,
please contact Simon & Schuster Special Sales at
1-866-506-1949 or business@simonandschuster.com.

The Simon & Schuster Speakers Bureau can bring authors to your live event. For
more information or to book an event, contact the Simon & Schuster Speakers
Bureau at 1-866-248-3049 or visit our website at www.simonspeakers.com.

Interior design by Davina Mock-Maniscalco

Manufactured in the United States of America

10 9 8 7 6 5 4 3 2 1

Library of Congress Cataloging-in-Publication Data is available.

ISBN 978-1-5011-8989-0
ISBN 978-1-5011-8990-6 (ebook)

INTRODUCTION

When *The Wait* was published in 2016, we had no idea how many people were going to read the book. We wanted to tell our story of deliberately choosing celibacy until marriage and the many ways God blessed us through and because of it. We hoped that our story would encourage people and inspire them to trust that waiting, rather than giving in to instant gratification, would lead to stronger relationships and deeper faith in God.

We were blown away by the way God used that book, and we are humbled to have been a part of the work He is doing. A number of readers have told us how the book inspired and encouraged them. We love hearing these stories, but it is God who deserves all the glory here. We didn't invent the concept of waiting. We just shared the way it blessed us.

Here's the thing, though. Even though we know The Wait works, it's not always fun. And even when you really want to obey God and trust in His timing, it can be extremely challenging to make the choice to wait each and every day.

That's where this book comes in. In this daily devotional, we've broken *The Wait* into short daily readings.

That way, you can think and pray about a short section of the book and really work on applying it to your life *that day*. We've also added a scripture for each day, as well as a question for reflection and a short prayer. This book can be used individually, or you and a partner can read it together. Our hope is that these short sections will allow you to grow closer to God and will deepen your commitment to wait, day by day—knowing that every day is a day of healing, hope, and wholeness.

During our marriage, we have both been blessed to work on some incredible projects and see our careers grow. But what's most incredible is the perspective that time brings. From where we stand now, we can see the ways God was preparing us through that time of waiting. Now we can see how the strengths and skills we learned in that period of obedience—such as patience, and trust, and faith that we want the best for each other—have equipped us for the challenges of married life.

We pray that these daily devotions will deepen your faith in God and help lead you through your Wait and into the blessings God has for you on the other side.

DeVon and Meagan, 2017

THE
WAIT
DEVOTIONAL

WHAT IS THE WAIT, EXACTLY?

The LORD is good to those who wait for
Him, to the person who seeks Him.
—Lamentations 3:25 NASB

As you begin this journey, you're probably asking yourself just exactly what is The Wait?

The Wait is a conscious choice to pursue delayed gratification in the areas of life specifically related to relationships. It's a decision to get your mind right, to figure out who you want to be and what you want out of life, and to use your time and energy to become the best version of yourself. Put simply:

> *To Wait is to delay the temptation for instant gratification in relationships in order to get what you really want in life and become the person you truly want to be.*

That starts with saying no to sex. The Wait isn't 100 percent about sex, but that's where it begins. So, let's be really, really clear on this:

> *One of the keys to practicing The Wait is giving up sex.*

For many Christians and non-Christians alike, the idea of giving up sex is too outrageous and impossible to consider. We get that. Yet based on our experience, we still believe that practicing The Wait until marriage will set you up for success and align you with God's perfect will for your life in all areas.

We are living proof . . . The Wait works.

> Now that you have a clear definition for what The Wait is, what are your thoughts? How do you think society—or at least your circle of it—views the concept of The Wait?

Lord God, while the idea of waiting is nothing new to You, it's not a popular one in this world today. Open up my mind to Your truth as I work through this study and learn to wait for Your will in all areas of my life. Amen.

....

....

....

....

....

....

....

....

....

....

....

A DIFFERENT WAY OF THINKING

God's will is for you to be holy,
so stay away from all sexual sin.
—*1 Thessalonians 4:3* NLT

It's just a fact. Human beings love sex. We think about it, talk about, it, read about it, and spend a great deal of our time, energy, and money trying to get it. Because of this, sex makes us do some truly stupid things.

From a spiritual standpoint, the Bible says to "stay away from all sexual sin." But people (Christian or not) are going to have sex. We find our reasons and justifications. The faith-minded might rationalize that waiting doesn't apply if you're dating the one you believe you're going to marry. Physically, it's just hard to resist those hormones. And socially, even the mention of going without sex is met with snickers and stares.

There's nothing wrong with sex or sexuality. God created both for the enjoyment of married couples. But for too long, there's been an ugly stigma associated with sex, the church, and where it all fits in the world we live in. We're not sex experts, and The Wait isn't about religious reasons not to have sex. It's our story, and we want to share what has worked for us. When we took sex off the table, our minds were clearer, our access to God was crisper, and we were able to make better decisions in areas of our relationship that weren't related to sex at all. The Wait is about getting control of your life, reducing the dating drama, and avoiding desperate relationship choices so that you can make better decisions about your future.

Navigating the waters between the worldly pressures to have sex and the spiritual pressures to wait is challenging at best. What has proven to be most difficult for you? Where do you find your strength?

Lord, waiting—for anything, but especially for sex—is a very different way of thinking in today's world. Please guide and change my thoughts so that they become a reflection of Yours. Amen.

....
....
....
....
....
....
....
....
....
....

CHASING THE HIGH

Like a city whose walls are broken through
is a person who lacks self-control.
—*Proverbs 25:28* NIV

We are all human, so we all like gratification—the more instant, the better. And sex is probably the most compelling aspect of human gratification. It's such a powerful desire that outside of a proper healthy context it can cloud our judgment and cause us to make decisions that work against our own best self-interest. The untamed, untampered drive for sexual gratification has toppled empires, scuttled political careers, destroyed marriages, and squandered fortunes. Sex can be like a McLaren F1 race car: great in the right hands, but potentially disastrous when handled recklessly.

Sex can also become a gateway drug to all kinds of other choices intended to satisfy the need for quick pleasure: going out with that gorgeous girl even though you know she's a hot mess, spending the weekend at that dude's place even though you know you're not the only one, or having just one more drink even though you know it will impair your judgment.

When we chase the high of instant gratification, we often make choices that are irresponsible and based on poor reasoning . . . or no reasoning at all. It takes time and self-control to take in information, let people reveal their true character, be consistent and disciplined, and give conflicts time to work themselves out. Delaying gratification means working at becoming more self-aware. And it also means being humble enough to admit that our first impulses aren't always smart ones.

Has acting on a first impulse ever gotten you into an awkward, even dangerous situation or relationship? Before the next impulse comes along, develop a game plan now. What can you do to prompt yourself to stop and think before you act?

Holy Lord, teach me to stop and think rather than just rushing right along with my first impulse. Teach me to wait. Amen.

....
....
....
....
....
....
....
....
....

LOVE AND SEX: TWO SIDES OF THE SAME COIN

Each of you should learn to control your own
body in a way that is holy and honorable.
—*1 Thessalonians 4:4* NIV

At its heart, The Wait is about relationships, but there's simply no unwinding the connection between relationships and sexuality. Love and sex are the two sides of the same coin. When you have sex with someone outside of marriage, you're not just setting off a chain of chemical reactions in your brain that make you think they're a lot better for you than they probably are; you're also giving that person a part of your spirit. You are leaving the person a piece of yourself and taking a part of him or her with you. So each sex partner becomes a part of your future. Does this make you think twice about who you choose—and have chosen—to get into bed with?

Strong relationships aren't built solely on physical or sexual attraction. They're built on good judgment. How many times have you become caught up with someone based mostly on sexual attraction? How have those relationships ended?

Notice that we don't have to ask *if* they've ended, because they don't last. They can't. Before too long, the hormonal haze clears and all that matters is character, integrity, intelligence, values, spirituality, and self-esteem. A person who doesn't have enough of those to suit you is a person you can't tolerate for long.

Delaying gratification and getting greater control over your behavior are the keys to finally finding the life and the peace that you hunger for.

> Are there patterns in your life—in who you are dating and pursuing—that are sabotaging you? How might delaying gratification and controlling your behavior help you find the life and peace you're seeking?

Lord, sometimes it's so easy to confuse love and attraction. Use this practice of The Wait to help me not only learn to control my own behavior but also learn discernment. Amen.

....
....
....
....
....
....
....
....
....

A man shall leave his father and his mother, and be
joined to his wife; and they shall become one flesh.
—Genesis 2:24 NASB

No matter how deep our faith and how intense our de-
votion and duty to God, we're still human, and human beings tend to be like twelve-year-olds when it comes
to the topic of sex. (LOL.)

Sex is pleasurable. Sex between two people who love
each other body and soul is transcendent. But more often
than not, that's not the kind of sex most people are having.
A good friend of ours once said to us, "I'm not getting
married until I have what you guys have." That's flatter-
ing and humbling, but it's also a reflection on how hard it
is to find compatibility.

The Wait is not anti-sex. The two of us are not anti-
sex. To be anti-sex would pretty much be the same as
being anti-God. God created sex, and we fully advocate
the joy of experiencing it the way He intended. What we
do know is that we've seen and known a lot of people
whose higher aspirations for love, family, and success have
landed on the rocks because they put the pursuit of sex before anything else.

The question "to have sex or not to have sex?" is at the

heart of The Wait. We can tell you that we saw incredible and undeniable grace come into our relationship when we decided to remain committed to celibacy before marriage. But ultimately, the question of whether or not to have sex is one that you have to answer for yourself.

> Take some time to answer "The Question" for yourself. Will you wait for marriage before having sex, and why? Are your reasons important enough to you to carry through with this commitment—even when it requires sacrifice?

Lord, You created sex to be a wonderful and amazing thing— in its proper time and place. Strengthen me as I commit to waiting for that time and place. Amen.

....
....
....
....
....
....
....
....
....
....

WHAT DO YOU DESERVE?

Praise be to the God and Father of our Lord Jesus
Christ, who has blessed us in the heavenly realms
with every spiritual blessing in Christ.
—*Ephesians 1:3* NIV

When you're beginning The Wait, it can be really beneficial to take some time to be alone and get used to the idea of not having sex and resisting temptation. This is a time to take stock of who you are, what you want, and why you've been having relationship troubles. That's wisdom. The world isn't going to end if you excuse yourself from the dating scene for a while. The right girls or guys will still be out there. But before you rejoin them, answer three very important questions for yourself:

- What relationship pattern do I want to break?

- What kind of person do I want in my life?

- What do I deserve?

The last one is the most important. We ask ourselves what we *want*, but we rarely ask ourselves what we *deserve*. When we forget to ask, we're more likely to approach relationships from a place of need and insufficiency. If you've spent years dating the same messed-up people, putting up with the same drama, and recovering from the same hysterical fights and awful breakups, ask yourself why. Was it because you felt, deep down, that was all you deserved? We're here to tell you that you deserve more. You're a child of God, an important player in manifesting God's will in the world. You deserve respect, fulfillment, joy, and the kind of profound, real love that comes only when you get to know someone's spirit and when you love yourself enough to let that person love you.

As a child of God, what do you deserve? Are you dating and living in a way that will bring you what you deserve? What might you need to change?

Lord, before You bring that special someone into my life, help me learn to truly love myself—so that I can then better love my future spouse. Amen.

....

....

....

....

....

....

....

....

....

STRATEGIC PATIENCE

We also pray that you will be strengthened
with all his glorious power so you will have all
the endurance and patience you need.
—Colossians 1:11 NLT

While *waiting* may sound passive, the truth is that The Wait is anything but passive. You're not sitting on your hands and hoping that things will turn out all right. You're making deliberate, positive choices that change who you are and how your mind works. You're also taking the resources you've been spending to chase after sexual gratification and using them instead to improve yourself in body, mind, and spirit.

We call this "strategic patience." You're not putting your life on hold; instead, you're taking all the time and attention that you've been projecting outward and turning it inward. From this perspective, you can finally see that hurling yourself into the path of potentially romantic relationships hasn't brought you any closer to what you want. It's time to try a different approach by working on becoming the best version of yourself.

Practicing strategic patience means understanding the difference between the two types of waiting:

1. Waiting that you choose.

2. Waiting that you have no choice about.

With the first, you're in control; with the second, you resent control being taken from you. The Wait is about changing your view of circumstances from the second type of waiting into the first. Instead of feeling resentful and angry when the pursuit of your desires hits a wall, think, "Okay, since I'm already waiting, I'm going to choose to use this time productively." Your circumstances haven't changed, but how you see them certainly has. Just like that, you transform yourself from passive victim into active collaborator with God.

> Are you choosing to wait, or are you waiting because you have no choice? How does the type of waiting affect your commitment to The Wait?

Lord, I know that I am in this season of waiting for a reason. Please guide me through it and use it to make me more faithful to You and Your plans for me. Amen.

....

....

....

....

THE WAIT IS NOT ...

Wait for the LORD; be strong
and take heart and wait for the LORD.
—Psalm 27:14 NIV

The Wait is a deliberate choice and an active commitment. Not only is The Wait *not* passive, but it is also not . . .

- *A punishment*. God isn't making you spend time alone as payback for some previous sin.

- *Forever*. We understand that not having sex is hard and could make a month feel like a year. But tell us this: What's the longest time in recent years that you've gone without sex against your will. Days? Weeks? Months? Years? Could you do that again, this time because you choose to?

- *Putting your life on hold*. Hardly. Now you have time and bandwidth to work on you. There are definitely times when fast, aggressive action is required to get what you want. You can still practice The Wait while you're actively going after all God has for you in life.

- *Weird*. We want to take the stigma away from waiting. What's bizarre about valuing yourself, your body, and your God over all else? Especially if you've already been through the pain of multiple bad breakups, there's nothing weird about waiting, no matter what anyone else says.

The most important thing to remember is that The Wait isn't powerless. Though you might not see it, God has His hand on your life during this time, rearranging the scenery in order to set you up for good things to come.

Look at that list again. Does one (or more) of those things resonate with you? Can you now see how The Wait is meant to be a blessing and not a curse?

Lord, thank You for Your presence and Your work in my life. Help me to trust in You while I wait. Amen.

....

....

....

....

....

....

....

....

A CULTURE OF SEX

I do not understand the things I do. I do not do
what I want to do, and I do the things I hate.
—*Romans 7:15* NCV

When we talk about The Wait and suggest that people consider going without sex, we get stares of horror. Many people can't even fathom going without sex for three months, much less years. On the male side, a lot of men have bought into the false idea that says that being a man means chasing lots of women. In that scenario, a man's worth has nothing to do with his character, morals, or integrity. It becomes reduced to how many women he sleeps with.

As for women, our culture tells them that their sexuality is one of the most important things they have to offer and then shames them for displaying it. It's really not surprising that sex provokes insecurity and internal conflicts. The unchecked premarital pursuit of sex can debase and objectify us, drive us farther away from God's plan for our life, and expose us to incurable STDs, unplanned pregnancies, and tons of emotional trauma. So why is it that more of us don't just stop?

Well, we like sex. We crave it. Faced with celibacy, we rationalize. We say, "I don't know how to be celibate." Or,

"We weren't meant to abstain." The problem is that what we should do is not what we want to do. It's a perfect example of instant gratification at war with delayed gratification. But by committing to The Wait, you can win that war and claim the prize of God's blessings on your life and your relationship.

> There are a lot of false ideas about sex in today's culture. What is the one false idea that has had the greatest—and most negative—impact on your life?

Lord, You know my heart, and You know I want to do what is right. Help me to resist the temptations this world throws at me. Amen.

....
....
....
....
....
....
....
....
....
....
....

TAKING SEX OUT OF THE EQUATION: DEVON'S TAKE

*"Seek the Kingdom of God above all else, and live
righteously, and he will give you everything you need."*
—*Matthew 6:33* NLT

While we both agreed that we needed to take sex out of the equation in order to be the people we truly wanted to be, we discovered that truth independently.

I had made a commitment of celibacy long before I met Meagan. When we got married, I had been celibate for over ten years. What motivated the commitment was the same thing that made me keep it. I was preaching about living a life that put the Lord first, and then I was going out and living a life that was the opposite of the discipline I was teaching. Trying to be two people started tearing me apart. The desire for peace and harmony within myself was a motivator to choose no sex.

I asked myself, "What if what I was doing with this other woman disqualified me for the full manifestation of the call that God has on my life? Would it be worth it?" Of course not! No sex is worth that! I could not reconcile the idea that at the end of my life God might say, "Here's what I had planned for you, but because you showed yourself unworthy, I couldn't do all I wanted to do in your life." I was not prepared to take that risk. Whatever my purpose is in this life, I didn't want anything to get in the way of that.

DeVon found himself asking if the things he was doing were disqualifying him for the "full manifestation of the call" that God placed on his life. Are you doing things that might disqualify you from God's call?

Lord, open my eyes to see the things that are keeping me from Your full blessings in my life. And please give me wisdom and strength to change those things. Amen.

....

....

....

....

....

....

....

....

....

....

....

....

TAKING SEX OUT OF THE EQUATION: MEAGAN'S TAKE

"Blessed are those who hunger and thirst for
righteousness, for they will be filled."
—Matthew 5:6 NIV

I got saved when I was twelve and lost my virginity when I was nineteen. As a Christian, I felt a strong conviction about not having sex, but like most of us, I made excuses and swept those convictions under the rug. And in some relationships, I tried hard to abstain; in others, I just guiltily went with the flow because I had failed miserably, so what was the point? I repeated the same painful patterns in my relationships over and over, but I didn't connect that to sex for a long time.

Finally, I knew I had to make a commitment to take sex off the table. I knew I couldn't do the same thing and expect a different result. My life was an emotional mess. Going celibate helped me clean it up in all areas (even areas where sex played no part). If I hadn't done that, I doubt that DeVon and I would have come together as husband and wife.

DeVon and I took a calculated risk: we would forgo physical pleasure so that we could really get to know each other's minds, hearts, and spirits and confirm that God was truly bringing us together. It wasn't always easy. But by waiting, we fell in love with each other as whole people, and the promised payoff has been a life filled with not just joy but the peace that comes with knowing we're firmly in the center of God's purpose.

Are you guilty of repeating the same mistakes while expecting a different result? Ask God to show you the things you need to change in your life—and then commit to changing them.

Lord, please keep me firmly fixed in the center of Your will. Help me to remove from my life those things that separate me from You and Your blessings. Amen.

....
....
....
....
....
....
....
....
....
....
....

CELIBACY... AND WHAT YOU DON'T KNOW ABOUT IT

And so, dear brothers and sisters, I plead with you to give
your bodies to God because of all he has done for you.
Let them be a living and holy sacrifice—the kind he will
find acceptable. This is truly the way to worship him.
—Romans 12:1 NLT

Maybe you have been getting some pretty clear signals from God about trying celibacy, but you don't want to go there. You think you'll be shunned or treated like some sort of freak. But there's probably a lot you don't know about celibacy:

- *More people are practicing it than you might think.* According to the Centers for Disease Control and Prevention and the National Institutes of Health, about 5 million couples in America currently remain celibate until their honeymoons.

- *Celibacy is about the mind as much as it is about the body.* Being celibate isn't just about pushing down hormonal needs. It's choosing to discipline the mind and think of the benefits you seek. The urges will still be there, make no mistake. But once you reframe sex as a choice, you can reframe celibacy as a commitment that will help you get the things you want.

- *Celibacy isn't about shame or moral judgment.* We are not anti-sex, but some people are. And they judge those who have sex out of wedlock as morally inferior. Do not listen to those people. Shame and the fear of being judged are the wrong reasons to practice The Wait.

- *Sex isn't sinful.* Sometimes people of faith have strange, outdated ideas about what sex is. God created the sexual act, and God-ordained sex between two people who are committed to each other in marriage, who know each other fully and are giving of themselves to each other, body and spirit—that is sanctified.

How might choosing to view sex as a choice and celibacy as a commitment help you gain power over your sexual urges?

Lord, this life is filled with so many choices. Teach me to make the choices that please You and draw me closer to You, especially in my relationships. Amen.

....

....

....

SIGNS

They were convinced by the power of miraculous signs
and wonders and by the power of God's Spirit.
—*Romans 15:19* NLT

One thing we've learned in our experiences with The Wait is that God won't leave you guessing. He will send you signs that it's time to slow down, quiet your mind, and work on yourself while He labors on your behalf. But it's up to you to read the signs that it's time to wait. They include:

- A breakup

- Physical or mental or emotional exhaustion

- Negative or hurtful people leaving your life

- The feeling of being lost or purposeless

- An opportunity to go on a long trip or retreat

- The awareness that you've been repeating the same relationship mistakes for years

- Persistent frustration and lack of peace

Not all of God's signs are enjoyable. Some are unpleasant or painful. But if that's what it takes to get your atten-

26

tion, it's worth it. Pay attention to the events and patterns in your life. Is God telling you to wait? If you haven't been listening, now is a good time to start. If not, you might squander time that you'll never get back.

> Has God placed signs in your life? Have you heeded or ignored them? What has the result been?

Holy Lord, open my eyes to see and my ears to hear the signs You place in my life. And then help me, Lord, to follow those signs. Amen.

....
....
....
....
....
....
....
....
....
....
....
....
....
....

YEAH ... IT'S ABOUT MARRIAGE

Many claim to have unfailing love,
but a faithful person who can find?
—Proverbs 20:6 NIV

Is The Wait only about waiting until marriage?

Yes. We do believe that most people's lives and relationships would be stronger and more joyful if they waited for sex until marriage. On the other hand, many people, no matter how strong their faith, will probably have sex or continue to before marriage. To ignore that would not only be dismissive but could be viewed as borderline delusional. Just like you, we live in the real world, where we try every day to live as spiritual beings dealing with the challenges of our flesh, so we do understand.

However, even with that understanding, we are confident that saving sex until after marriage will yield the best results, both for you as an individual and for you and your partner. That's what we did. We can speak to the blessings firsthand. We've seen God do amazing things in our lives that we believe are directly connected to putting Him first in all areas of our life—including our sex life.

We get that some people's strong desire for sex and their differing perspectives on premarital sex might make them unlikely to wait until marriage. That said, we believe that to gain all the blessings connected to The Wait, celibacy should continue until you make that vow of lasting commitment.

So that's our perspective; that's our focus. We're not denying the real world; we're just reflecting on the way that the two of us navigated the real world and our own sexual desires to find real, deep, authentic love: no sex until marriage.

> Take some time to think about your commitment to The Wait. Is it until marriage? Write out a statement of your commitment and your reasons for deciding to take this step.

Lord, this commitment I'm making is not only to myself but also to You and my future spouse. Help me to honor it. Amen.

....

....

....

....

....

....

....

....

....

THE BLESSINGS OF THE WAIT

Wait for the LORD and keep His way, and He
will exalt you to inherit the land.
—*Psalm 37:34 NASB*

Giving up sex can seem impossible, but believe us, it's worth it. The things that happened in the months after our marriage were not things we could have planned or even thought we deserved. Putting God first and making Him the foundation of our union has been not only the best personal decision we've ever made but also the best decision for our careers and lives.

DEVON: When you're disciplined, obedient, and faithful, God will bring His plan A, the best destiny you could imagine. That's what I wanted. I knew that if I had remained undisciplined and continued to make bad choices, God would still be a benevolent God. He would bring me something from plan B, plan C, or plan D, but that wasn't enough. I said, "Lord, I want it all." And God has delivered above and beyond anything I could have hoped or asked for.

MEAGAN: Everything in my life has changed dramatically since I stopped picking and choosing which parts of the Bible I would follow. I stopped saying, "I'm going to do *this* by the book, but I'm going to do *that* the way I want to do it." When I stopped that and I focused on the hardest thing, which is sex, I literally watched everything in my life and career change.

Waiting for sex wasn't easy, but no important thing is ever easy. It was a sacrifice, but a worthwhile one. And then finally enjoying sex after our marriage became the consummation of something holy.

Have you ever been willing to settle for plan B, C, or D because you weren't willing to make the sacrifice necessary to obtain God's plan A? Do you pick and choose which parts of the Bible you will follow? How have these choices affected your relationships, your career, your life?

Lord, I want Your plan A. Show me the kind of life I need to live—the sacrifices I need to make—in order to bring Your very best into my life. Amen.

....

....

....

....

VIRTUE AND VICE

Desire without knowledge is not good—
how much more will hasty feet miss the way!
—Proverbs 19:2 NIV

Influential philosopher St. Thomas Aquinas said:

> *A person is said to be patient . . . because he acts in*
> *a praiseworthy manner by enduring things which*
> *hurt him here and now and is not unduly saddened*
> *by them.*

We consider patience a virtue and impatience a vice, but why?

In part, it's because a patient disposition tends to give us a healthier perspective on the ups and downs of daily living. Because we're not expecting everything to come our way overnight, we keep the big picture in mind. We're less likely to become angry or depressed at life's trivial setbacks. The impatient person, on the other hand, can't understand why everything isn't working out as planned and is more likely to react to a minor misfortune by becoming frustrated, giving up, or doing something foolish.

Perhaps that's why the Proverbs declare that it is "better to be patient than powerful" (16:32 NLT).

Would you consider yourself a patient person in general? What about in your sexual—or potentially sexual—relationships? Does this create a positive or negative impact on your relationships?

Lord, I've often heard it's dangerous to pray for patience, but I do pray for that now. Teach me to wait for Your blessings, Your way, and Your will. Amen.

....
....
....
....
....
....
....
....
....
....
....
....
....
....
....
....
....

CELIBACY VERSUS ABSTINENCE

"Small is the gate and narrow the road that
leads to life, and only a few find it."
—Matthew 7:14 NIV

I t's important to draw a clear distinction between celibacy and abstinence. Most people think they're the same thing. They're not. *Abstinence* is simply refraining from sex; it's the absence of something with no greater meaning behind it. To us, *celibacy* is refraining from sex because of a vow or faith; it's abstinence with a purpose. You might abstain from sex involuntarily, because you're not in a relationship. Celibacy is never involuntary. It's always the result of a conscious, deliberate choice. That's an important distinction.

The Wait is about celibacy because to us, celibacy is something you go into with your eyes open, fully expecting to gain something from the experience. It's about saying, "I'm becoming." On the other hand, in our culture abstinence is something grudging, something forced upon young people, for example, by well-meaning parents or well-meaning ministries. It's about saying, "You will not." But there's not always a purpose or learning associated with it.

When we talk about celibacy, the last thing we're doing is telling you to ignore sex. Just the opposite. We're suggesting that you acknowledge its power and your own desire. That way, if you choose to go without sex, you'll do so with your eyes open, understanding the realities and risks of having sex and not having it. Celibacy and The Wait complement each other.

What do you believe are the key differences between celibacy and abstinence? Which are you practicing and why?

Lord, I know that there is a way You have planned for me. Help me to honor You with every choice I make. Amen.

....
....
....
....
....
....
....
....
....
....
....
....

WHEN YOU'RE TYPE-A

The heart of man plans his way,
but the Lord establishes his steps.
—Proverbs 16:9 ESV

Type-A personalities may struggle more than others with The Wait. They often see it as disempowering or fatalistic. So many times we hear self-help tropes like, "Go for what you want in life" and "Successful people make things happen; unsuccessful people watch things happen." That sort of one-size-fits-all wisdom sounds enticing until you realize that it could leave God completely out of the picture.

For some scriptural perspective, look at Isaiah 40:30–31 (NASB), which reads,

Though youths grow weary and tired,
And vigorous young men stumble badly,
Yet those who wait for the Lord
Will gain new strength;
They will mount up with wings like eagles,
They will run and not get tired,
They will walk and not become weary.

Yes, even vigorous young men and women—those Type-A's, so impatient and confident in their ability to choose the right person or right path—will stumble and wear out without God's guidance to give them strength.

Do you have a Type-A personality that's trying to take over? Are you following your own plans or the Lord's? When you pray, are you asking or telling? What difference would that make?

Dear Lord, I never want to leave You out of the picture of my life. Teach me to seek Your will—and surrender to it—each and every day. Amen.

....
....
....
....
....
....
....
....
....
....
....
....
....
....

ESCAPING THE LOVE MAZE

God blesses those who patiently endure testing and
temptation. Afterward they will receive the crown of
life that God has promised to those who love him.
—*James 1:12* NLT

Running through love's maze—chasing one bad relationship after another—discourages not just the body but also the spirit. The word *discourage* says it all: it involves a loss of courage. After a while, you don't have the fortitude to face another first date or relationship. It's exhausting.

Showing restraint and letting God reveal your next step, however, is like plugging into an emotional and spiritual power plant. As Isaiah 40:30–31 says, you can run and not get tired. You're not just free of the maze but free of the unspoken mandate that you must find your life's partner and life's purpose *right now*. You're on nobody's schedule but your own, and you have God to help you figure out what to do next.

In the entertainment business, we've learned that the key to any good movie is tension. Whether you're waiting for two characters to share their first kiss or for the heroine to escape from the serial killer, what moves the story is the tension between what the main character wants and the obstacles he or she must overcome to get it. That same tension gives The Wait its power.

The Wait takes the tension between instant and delayed gratification and turns it into energy. In the Bible, giving in to the temptations of instant gratification inevitably leads to ruin. (See Eden, Garden of.) Delayed gratification, on the other hand, leads to reward. (See Joseph.) The fact is this: waiting for what you want floods your life with potential energy. So why not wait?

> Has the pursuit of love ever felt like being trapped in a maze? Keeping the principles of The Wait in mind, what would escaping that maze look like for you?

Lord, it's so easy to give in to the here and now. Help me, instead, to slow down, to seek out Your guidance, and to wait for Your reward. Amen.

....

....

....

....

....

....

....

....

MORE THAN MARSHMALLOWS

*"The master answered, 'You did well. You are a good
and loyal servant. Because you were loyal with small
things, I will let you care for much greater things.'"*
—Matthew 25:21 NCV

The benefits of delayed gratification were perhaps most memorably demonstrated in what's become known as the famous Stanford marshmallow experiment. In the 1960s, a Stanford University professor named Walter Mischel started experimenting with hundreds of children around four and five years old to see how long they could delay their own gratification.

In the experiment, a researcher brought each child into a room and sat down across a table from him or her. On the table he placed a marshmallow. Then he told each child that he would leave the room for fifteen minutes. The children who did not eat the marshmallow would get a second marshmallow when the researcher came back. If a child ate the marshmallow, he or she wouldn't get any more.

As you might expect, most kids ate the marshmallows. A few didn't. But the interesting part of the study came when the researchers followed the kids over the next forty years as they grew into adults. Kids who were able to delay gratification grew up to be more successful in almost every area of life: lower rates of obesity, better social skills, higher SAT scores, you name it. They were simply better at life than the kids who gave in to instant gratification.

If you've never been disciplined enough to deny yourself short-term pleasure in favor of the big picture, The Wait is your chance to develop this skill. Doing so can increase your chances of success in your career, your relationships, and everything in between.

> Be honest: would you pass the marshmallow test? What are the "marshmallows" that most tempt you to give in to instant gratification? How can you work to remove their power?

Lord, please give me the strength to look ahead to the greater rewards waiting for me rather than give in to the temptations of today. Amen.

....
....
....
....
....
....
....
....

THE DANGERS OF "WHAT-I-WANT-WHEN-I-WANT IT"

If any of you needs wisdom, you should ask God
for it. He is generous to everyone and will give
you wisdom without criticizing you.
—James 1:5 NCV

The "I-want-what-I-want-when-I-want-it" mentality offers a relatively neat, if unfavorable, summary of our culture. But when we base our actions on this drive, we don't see clearly. We make decisions based on lust, greed, envy, or fear, and more often than not such choices cause destruction in our lives. Sometimes the harm is temporary, as in a bad breakup that's painful for a few weeks but survivable. Other times the damage is permanent, such as when quick decisions result in disease, depression, or an unplanned pregnancy and change the course of our lives forever.

The fact is that when we're focused primarily on satisfying our immediate desires, we're preventing ourselves from being the best people we can be. And one of the key elements of being the best people we can be is to be the healthiest person we can be—physically, as well as emotionally and spiritually. The short-term results of instant gratification might be fun, but in the long term we often damage our health and ourselves. Not to mention we can become like addicts chasing the next high. The Wait helps put reason and discernment back in charge. And it changes our mentality from "what I want" to "what God wants."

Think about the things you want in your life. Are you willing to sacrifice getting something "right now" in order to get what you really want later on down the road? More important, are you willing to sacrifice what you want for what God wants? Why is sacrifice key to The Wait?

Lord, change my heart so that what I want more than anything else is what You want. Amen.

....
....
....
....
....
....
....
....
....
....
....

AN UNEXPECTED BENEFIT

Am I now trying to win the approval of human beings, or of God? Or am I trying to please people? If I were still trying to please people, I would not be a servant of Christ.
—*Galatians 1:10 NIV*

Practicing The Wait has many advantages, from spiritual to emotional to physical, as well as relationships. But there's another big plus to delaying gratification and reining in your dating life that you might not expect:

The less available you are, the more fascinating you become.

We live in a culture where most people hurl themselves blindly into the path of every possible relationship. In that world, who's most interesting and desirable? The person who has the confidence not to date every warm body that comes along but instead is selective. Just as tension powers the action in the movies, it will do the same for you.

Regardless of where you are in your dating life, The Wait will work for you. Because ultimately, if your desire to please God is greater than your desire to please yourself, then God will bring you boundless blessings. Tether your will to wait to your desire to please God, and He will bless you and honor your commitment in ways that will surprise you. Such as making you even more fascinating to the opposite sex.

Why do you think that the less available you are, the more attractive you become? What role does confidence—in yourself, in God, and in His purpose for you—play in this?

Holy Lord, help me to seek to please You first, not myself, not others, and not this world. Amen.

....
....
....
....
....
....
....
....
....
....
....
....
....
....

THE WAIT AND ... YOUR CAREER

Whatever you do, work at it with all your heart, as
working for the Lord, not for human masters.
—*Colossians 3:23* NIV

The Wait is about sex, but it isn't *just* about sex. Your career is another area where practicing The Wait and delayed gratification can bring very real blessings to your life.

You might be chomping at the bit to get going, get climbing that ladder, and get the corner office, but you have only so much control. There are politics, the realities of advancement within an organization, and issues of training and education to deal with. Plus, sometimes it's just hard to know what you should really do with your life.

Waiting can be a great career strategy, because believe it or not, God honors your sacrifice. And let's face it, the decision to deny yourself and not have sex is a sacrifice. The two of us have witnessed firsthand how God has blessed our careers because we chose to honor Him in our relationship. As you practice The Wait, you can see a great acceleration and advancement in your purpose and career.

What are your career goals? While you are waiting, what is the next step you can take in reaching those goals?

Lord, You know my hope, my goals, my dreams. But I give them all to You and pray that You would shape them so that they rest completely in Your will. Amen.

....
....
....
....
....
....
....
....
....
....
....
....
....
....
....
....
....
....

TIME TO HEAL

He heals the brokenhearted and binds up their wounds.
—Psalm 147:3 NIV

God designed sex and love to be a power combination in marriage. However, when sex and love don't end in marriage—which describes the outcome of most sexual flings and love affairs—the result is oftentimes painful. When you're with someone God doesn't intend for you, pain of some sort is usually inevitable.

Many of us still bear the wounds and the sorrow from those lost loves or flings. But do we give ourselves time to heal? No, not typically. Suffering from post-traumatic relationship disorder, we follow the only prescription we know: we bury the feelings that we aren't ready to deal with, go into denial mode, and look for escape in other sexual relationships. But what we really need is time to process the pain we've gone through and properly heal so that we don't make the same mistakes again.

Celibacy is the heart and soul of The Wait because control over this area of instant gratification empowers you. It gives you control over so many other areas in your life—the same ones that may have led to a repetitive pattern of heartbreak, loneliness, wasted money, and wasted time. Reason number one to practice The Wait: it's a time to heal when the only one who matters is you.

> Think back over past failed relationships. Do you see any patterns of mistakes emerging? How will you use this time of waiting to break those patterns and allow yourself to heal?

Lord, heal my heart and my soul. Reveal my mistakes to me, and bless me with the wisdom and the courage to stop repeating them. Amen.

....
....
....
....
....
....
....
....
....
....
....
....
....

LETTING GOD HAVE CONTROL

*The LORD is my shepherd, I lack nothing. He makes me lie down
in green pastures, he leads me beside quiet waters, he refreshes
my soul. He guides me along the right paths for his name's sake.*
—Psalm 23:1–3 NIV

The Wait applies to every area of romantic life and relationships, from whom we choose to date to when to
get serious. In all these areas, people tend to try to make
things happen. We force the issue. We delude ourselves
into thinking that we alone can order the universe to our
liking if we just have the right look, income, or position.

The Wait reminds us that while we have the power of
choice, much of what happens in our life is still subject to
God's control. Our hands are on the wheel, but so are
God's. We can steer with Him, because we do have control
over our choices, our habits, and how we use the gifts
we've been given. Or we can try to take over. But when we
try to seize control, we usually find ourselves in a head-on
collision with something or someone that God was trying
to steer us away from.

Practicing The Wait is a chance to heal, clear your
head, do some important self-assessment, and position
yourself to receive peace, love, and wisdom. It's an opportunity to take a break from the frantic feeling that you

have to make things happen or they won't happen at all. The Wait is about having faith that God is working on your behalf to bring you the right blessings at the right time.

Are you allowing God to steer your life? If not, what's stopping you? Write out your commitment to God, vowing to surrender control of your life to Him.

Holy Lord, You have promised to lead me, to guide me, and to refresh my soul. Help me to surrender completely to Your leading. Amen.

....

....

....

....

....

....

....

....

....

....

....

....

....

WAITING FOR THE BEST
VERSION OF YOURSELF

I praise you because I am fearfully and wonderfully made;
your works are wonderful, I know that full well.
—Psalm 139:14 NIV

There is a critical period between wanting and getting—that period is The Wait. It's when you quiet your mind and trust God. Relieved of the pressure to live the perfect life (whew!), you're free to reinvent yourself as the person you've always aspired to be—the person He intends you to be. For some, that means taking classes and working out. For others, it means reading Scripture and ridding themselves of toxic relationships. While waiting, you need to trust more than ever that God's got your back, then start making life choices that show you have your own back, too.

This isn't easy. We ache to find our life partners, so we push the issue. We date without employing critical thinking or prayer to help us determine if that person is worthy of our time. We stay in relationships that are way past their sell-by date. We say yes to quick marriages and then say yes to quick divorces. It's not making us any happier. In fact, it's making us more cynical, and loading us up with emotional baggage that we'll need to unpack years down the road.

But we don't have to give in to cynicism. The Wait creates the path for you to become the best version of yourself. You will grow into someone of greater wisdom, discernment, self-awareness, compassion, and empathy, and it's incredible how everything falls into place. It's as though God was always just around the corner, waiting to bless you when you found your way onto the right path.

Write out a word "sketch" of how you see the best version of yourself. What do you need to start/stop/do/change in order to become that best version of you?

Lord God, You created me with a plan and a purpose. Mold me into the person You created me to be. Amen.

....

....

....

....

....

....

....

....

For we are God's masterpiece. He has created us
anew in Christ Jesus, so we can do the good
things he planned for us long ago.
—*Ephesians 2:10* NLT

One of the most common regrets among couples who got married too soon is that they didn't get to live their lives as singles while they had the chance. That's sad, because there's nothing stopping you from living the life you want—the life that God wants you to live so you can learn all about yourself. While you're free of entanglements, you're also free for adventures, seeing the world, trying different jobs, and dating different people.

Sample some of these experiences while you're young and unencumbered:

- *Travel*. See as much of God's world as you can. It's a wondrous, thrilling place that will take you out of your comfort zone and show you new sides of yourself.

- *Serve*. There's no better time to do this than when you're single. Try many ways of serving until you find one that moves you: feeding the homeless, reading to children in hospitals, building homes for Habitat for Humanity, and so on.

- *Work for yourself.* Not everyone is cut out for self-employment, but if you've always wanted to try it, there's no time like the present.

- *Pursue your passion.* Whether your passion is music, dance, writing, acting, or art, it's part of you. Making a career out of that passion, however, takes a lot of work and sacrifice, and those are much easier to endure when you're single.

- *Relocate.* Always wanted to live in New York or Los Angeles? Go for it! That's a lot harder to do when you're with someone else.

When you're single, you can do what *you* want to do. So . . . what do you want to do? Now, take the first step toward doing it.

Lord, it's easy to focus on what I don't have —a spouse. But help me, instead, to see all the opportunities that I do have, and show me which ones to follow. Amen.

....

....

....

*Whatever is good and perfect is a gift coming down to us
from God our Father, who created all the lights in the
heavens. He never changes or casts a shifting shadow.*
—James 1:17 NLT

Practicing The Wait has paid big rewards for us. Our marriage is a powerful, mutually respectful relationship. We know how very much God has blessed us, but that wouldn't have happened without The Wait. Practicing it has improved our lives in more ways than we can count:

- *We're more patient.* Our experience of waiting and watching God bring us together has taught us the incredible virtue of patience. There are some things that we can't make happen. Other things will happen, but only in their own time when certain conditions have been met.

- *We're free to be ourselves.* We spent more time on dates talking about what we liked, didn't like, were offended by, you name it. We've seen each other at our weirdest, silliest, most ornery and disagreeable, most vulnerable, and most hurtful. And guess what? We've both made the decision to love the whole package.

- *We have a home within a home.* We both can work incredibly long hours in demanding professions. And when our wells are dry, we have someplace to go and someone to go to that is ours, our haven, our center of peace. Home is about the person more than the place.

- *We've made peace with the past.* The worst thing about past pain is that it makes you doubt your wisdom to make sound choices. As we confronted our demons, we decided to let go of the guilt of previous mistakes and not allow our past to control our future.

> As you look at this list of blessings, are any—or all—of them things you want in your life? Are you willing to sacrifice the instant gratification of sex to get them?

Dear Lord, when temptation seems so strong, remind me of the blessings that I am waiting for. Amen.

....

....

....

....

....

GETTING WHAT YOU WANT

*Blessed is the one . . . whose delight is in the law of the LORD,
and who meditates on his law day and night. That person is like
a tree planted by streams of water, which yields its fruit in season
and whose leaf does not wither—whatever they do prospers.*
—*Psalm 1:1–3 NIV*

One of the most important reasons people choose to delay gratification is also the simplest: *it helps us get what we want.* Successful dieters resist the temptation to overeat because they like seeing a slimmer reflection, not because they love watching what they eat all day long. People who sacrifice to save cushy retirement nest eggs do it mostly because they want to have money in their older years, not because they don't have a desire to spend money. Our desires are powerful drivers of our decision-making process, which helps or hinders us from getting what we want most.

The two of us are not naive. The promise of becoming the person God wants you to be isn't necessarily enough to change behavior by itself, particularly when it comes to love and sex, areas where we humans are prone to stepping on our own toes. If you want to wait to date, have sex, get married, or do anything else purely out of deep religious or moral conviction, we admire and respect that. But the *desire* to wait is different from the *ability* to wait, and it's a lot easier to remain celibate and delay gratification if you know you're doing it because it brings concrete benefits.

As you seek to practice The Wait, what concrete benefits are you hoping will result from delaying gratification? Does this help you stay faithful to your commitment to The Wait?

Lord God, create in me a desire to wait, and please strengthen me in my ability to wait. Amen.

THE WAIT AND ... FINANCES

*And my God will meet all your needs according
to the riches of his glory in Christ Jesus.*
—Philippians 4:19 *NIV*

Oh, that crazy consumer culture. We fuel a trillion-dollar economy because we just can't help instantly gratifying our insatiable desires for new cars, shoes, and bigger flat-screen televisions. It's no wonder we Americans save only a small percentage of our incomes.

Waiting is a powerful principle when it comes to your dating relationships. But it is also a powerful principle when it comes to your relationship with money—more to the point, to spending less of it and saving more. If you follow the precepts it's pretty simple: don't give in to your hunger for a shiny new toy. Save that money instead for the purchases that will provide for your future, like a home, an IRA, or a 401(k). Or just stick it in a savings account so that in five years you can take your Wait-met spouse on the honeymoon of a lifetime.

There's nothing too complicated here. The Wait and money means focusing on long-term versus short-term goals. Want to buy a house? Saving is a must. That doesn't mean you can't still eat out and have nice things, but you might have to do that more selectively than before. Decide what's important and manage your money accordingly.

> Write out your financial goals. Now, take some time to create a plan for how to achieve those goals. Do you need to avoid certain spending traps? Or perhaps say no to your wants in order to save more and to give more?

Lord, every material blessing I have comes from You. Help me to use these blessings to honor You. Amen.

....

....

....

....

....

....

....

....

....

....

....

....

....

SAYING NO

So flee youthful passions and pursue righteousness,
faith, love, and peace, along with those who
call on the Lord from a pure heart.
—*2 Timothy 2:22 ESV*

Psychologists have found that the ability to say no to immediate, short-term pleasures in favor of lasting ones down the line is linked to better mental and physical health, greater academic success, and more refined social abilities. Why does delaying gratification make us better people? We believe it's all about how our minds and bodies are programmed to see pleasure.

Every day is a contest between pleasures of the flesh and of the spirit. Fleshly pleasures are about immediate satisfaction of our desires through things like food, sex, spending money, feeling superior to other people, and so on. We call these pleasures SEE: Short-term External Experiences. You might have noticed that SEEs have a lot in common with addictive behaviors. These quick-fix experiences that give us instant gratification can also control our behavior and lead us to make destructive choices.

Spiritual pleasures, on the other hand, evoke our highest qualities, the ones that move us to do the will of God and align with who He wants us to be. Generosity, discipline, fidelity, compassion, self-sacrifice, acting ethically and honestly—these are some of the pleasures that we call LIP: Long-term Internal Processes. Cultivating these qualities often means delaying gratification, and the process affects us mostly in our minds and spirits. When we do the right thing or care for others before ourselves, we get a soul-deep sense of pleasure and accomplishment that's nothing like the superficial pleasures of the flesh.

What are your greatest SEEs? Your greatest LIPs? Do you agree that the pleasures of the long term far outweigh the pleasures of the short term? What is an example from your own life?

Lord, help me to look beyond today and to look ahead to the blessings You have waiting for me tomorrow. Amen.

....

....

....

....

....

....

....

....

....

BALANCING SPIRIT AND FLESH

Those who live according to the flesh have their minds set
on what the flesh desires; but those who live in accordance
with the Spirit have their minds set on what the Spirit
desires. The mind governed by the flesh is death, but
the mind governed by the Spirit is life and peace.
—Romans 8:5–6 NIV

Emotionally and spiritually healthy people maintain a good balance between fleshly and spiritual pleasures. They date widely but don't sleep around. They enjoy material comforts but don't overspend. They live balanced lives by putting God first while still finding ways to enjoy His blessings. The trouble is, our culture works 24/7 to tell us that indulging in fleshly pleasure (instant gratification) is the better way to live. We've become *programmed* to favor the flesh over the Spirit.

This continuous, unbalanced practice of choosing the flesh over the Spirit can be dangerously self-destructive. For example, we have unprotected sex with people we barely know, abuse alcohol or drugs and call it fun, stay in dysfunctional relationships and call it love, and spend more money than we have and call it prosperity.

The greatest benefit of The Wait is that it *reprograms* us to find greater pleasure in choices that help us live according to the Spirit. This serves our long-term mental, emotional, and spiritual health. Take us as an example. By choosing to wait, we were able to appreciate the pleasure that came with listening to God, learning about ourselves, and breaking old patterns.

When you choose to deny the flesh in favor of the Spirit, you'll find that doing things in this way feels really good—and that giving in to the needs of the flesh starts to feel less desirable. Even better, the more you derive pleasure from Spirit-led decisions that make you stronger and more self-aware, the better choices you'll make.

How would putting God first bring balance to your life? What would putting God first look like for you? What changes would you need to make?

Holy Father, so much in this world tries to come between You and me. Help me to set aside this world and keep You first in my life. Amen.

CHOICES FOR LONG-TERM SUCCESS

*Choose this day whom you will serve . . . But as for
me and my house, we will serve the LORD.*
—*Joshua 24:15 ESV*

The essence of The Wait is developing the ability to derive more pleasure and peace from delaying gratification than you do from giving in to the hunger for instant gratification. By encouraging your spiritual development, you will make choices that reward you over the long term and improve your happiness in every area of your life.

What kind of choices can bring you greater pleasure and satisfaction than quick-fix pleasures of the flesh? Here are some examples:

- Maintaining a disciplined program of fitness

- Budgeting and saving money

- Praying and meditating consistently

- Being celibate, which eliminates distractions and improves vision, clarity, and discernment

- Helping others in need

- Mentoring and giving back

- Finding a church community that can help nurture you and give you support

Anytime you act with morality, restraint, good character, or strong discipline—when you do things that enhance instead of corrupt your spirit—you will enjoy tremendous peace, pride, and personal satisfaction. That's the kind of pleasure that lasts . . . and will fuel long-term success.

Look again at the list above, and choose an area to focus on this day and in the coming days. How might such a focus lead you to long-term success? Outline the steps of a plan to make that focus a habit in your life.

Lord, there is so much more to me—and to the person You created me to be—than sex. Teach me to become a whole and complete person, serving You and others, not just myself. Amen.

....

....

....

....

....

....

....

....

TAKE BACK YOUR POWER

God has not given us a spirit of fear and timidity,
but of power, love, and self-discipline.
—2 Timothy 1:7 NLT

You might not like to admit it, but the fact is that every time you give yourself to someone before marriage, you give that person your power. It's time to take your power back. It's time to take control of your decisions, which is where the real power lies.

Many times, the waiting periods in life come to us not by our own choice. Circumstances like a breakup or job loss force them on us. Instead of using these periods as opportunities to do the work we've needed to do, we use them to complain, throw a self-pity party, and spiral into depression. One of the many goals of The Wait is to motivate you to change your thinking about the unexpected seasons—to use periods of active waiting to sculpt your life into the shape you want.

It's true that God is the only one who knows the right time for a person or opportunity to appear in your life. However, *you* have control over how you prepare before that person or opportunity arrives—and how you respond afterward. God gives us all the raw material we will ever need to become the person He wants us to become, but it's up to us to do the cutting and polishing so that the true beauty and light of our character and God-intended destiny emerges.

Are you *actively* waiting? Identify an area of your life that needs some attention. What can you actively do to "cut and polish" that area, so that you are ready for the person God brings into your life?

Lord, show me the weaknesses in my life, and bless me with the wisdom, knowledge, and courage to strengthen them. Amen.

....
....
....
....
....
....
....
....
....
....
....
....
....
....
....

ANSWERING THE TOUGH QUESTIONS

*Whether you turn to the right or to the left, your ears will hear
a voice behind you, saying, "This is the way; walk in it."*
—Isaiah 30:21 NIV

When you are practicing The Wait, the time when nothing appears to be happening becomes your personal self-development laboratory. It's the time to reflect on what you've done wrong in the past so you can do things right in the future. And it's the time to ask some of the most challenging questions you'll ever confront:

- What's likely to happen and how can I be ready?

- What part did I play in the failure of my last relationship or opportunity?

- What negative patterns do I see myself repeating over and over?

- Am I pursuing opportunities that please my flesh over my spirit?

- What type am I attracted to? Am I attracted to people who aren't right for me?

- What emotions have sabotaged my relationships? Rage? Depression? Revenge?

- What traumas have I not worked through yet? Betrayal?

Evaluating your traumatic relationship's ups and downs productively is constructive action. Set aside the victim mentality—it just robs you of control and of the privilege of taking responsibility. Take your power back. By doing what needs to be done to avoid past mistakes (change your cell number, join a new gym, take an overdue vacation to clear your head, whatever), you prepare yourself for the incredible future God has in store for you.

Carve out some time to sit and really answer these questions. Perhaps even ask a good friend to help you honestly assess your past choices and relationships. Then take at least three concrete steps to address the issues you uncover.

Holy Lord, I look at my past and I know that my future needs to be different. Show me the path You want me to follow and the actions I need to take to get there. Amen.

....
....
....
....
....

WHAT A WOMAN FEARS ... "IF I DON'T SLEEP WITH HIM, I'LL LOSE HIM"

Let all who take refuge in you be glad; let them ever
sing for joy. Spread your protection over them, that
those who love your name may rejoice in you.
—Psalm 5:11 NIV

Let's be honest: there are some men who won't go along with a woman's vow to abstain until marriage. However, this isn't something you should fear. The right man will be open to waiting for the woman he loves and knows he is destined to be with. Here's a secret about men, ladies:

A man who says no to celibacy isn't making a state-
ment about you. It's about him.

Men's identity is closely tied to their sexuality. Many a man faced with a celibate relationship is going to worry that other men will make fun of him and think him less of a man because he's not getting any. He's going to say no to you because he's used to women who will offer sex as a way to keep him happy.

If you're compatible and really care about each other and he still bolts as soon as you suggest The Wait, he's really saying, "I'm not strong or evolved enough to go without sex." An admission like this might also reveal that he doesn't see a long-term future with you—a good thing to know so you don't waste more of your time.

A man leaving you over sex is a blessing, because it tells you that he wasn't meant to be your husband. On the other hand, if you ditch celibacy out of desperation to keep him, you could end up wasting years with the wrong person. Worse yet, you might marry a man whose lack of sexual discipline lays the foundation for infidelity down the line.

Have you ever acted on this fear—that if you didn't sleep with a man, you would lose him? In hindsight, was such a man worth keeping?

Lord, I know You have a plan for me—a plan to bring a wonderful and godly man into my life. Help me to trust in You and not give in to my fears. Amen.

....

....

....

....

....

....

....

....

....

WHAT A MAN FEARS...
LOOKING LIKE LESS

For what does it profit a man if he gains the
whole world and loses or forfeits himself?
—Luke 9:25 ESV

There's a lot of validation and pleasure in being part of a female-chasing pack of dudes. You get camaraderie, approval of your skills, and a built-in wingman on a Saturday night. It's appealing. Understood.

But here's the secret no one's talking about: almost every player knows that what he's doing is unhealthy and disrespectful to himself and women (because if another man was doing the same thing to his mother, sister, or daughter, he wouldn't stand for it). Guys know, deep down, that chasing sexual pleasure diminishes them and debases women. But the pressure of the pack—to fit in and get that fist-bump, you're-the-man approval—is powerful.

But if you're going to practice The Wait and do it right, you need to step up and be the leader. Say what none of your brothers will say: this isn't good for you and you're opting out. You're going celibate to prove that you're more than your sex drive. The guys will laugh it off as a joke at first. Then they'll be shocked and a little upset. Some might withdraw their validation, and you might panic and feel the need to retract your resolve.

Don't. Stick to your guns. Men respect strength, even if it's in something they disagree with. Your real friends will back your play, even if they don't get it. Once they see how it's giving you the time and focus to get your mind right, excel in your career, and get in shape, who will be laughing then?

> Do you ever feel the pressure of the pack? Has it led you to doing things you now regret? What is your plan for breaking free of that pressure?

Lord God, You are more powerful than anything here on earth or in the universe above. Fill me with that power, so that I may stand strong against the pressures to give in to temptation. Amen.

....
....
....
....
....
....
....
....

BREAKING THE CYCLE

*Do not forget my teaching, but keep my commands
in your heart, for they will prolong your life many
years and bring you peace and prosperity.*
—*Proverbs 3:1–2* NIV

There's great power in stepping back, looking at things with a clear head, and most important, breaking the cycle of repeated mistakes. You gain the perspective to make preparations that will lead to the outcomes you want, and you gain control during periods of your life that might seem uncontrollable. Here's a glimpse of how breaking the cycle looked in our lives:

MEAGAN: Actively deciding to wait was not about me finding my guy. It was about the fact that some of the relationships I had been in were destructive to who I was as a human being, and to who I wanted to be in God. I played a huge role in this as well. I knew better. Everything was in disarray, and I needed to let God put the pieces back together. It was time for me to take my relationship with God deeper and closer.

DeVON: When we're distracted by our drama, we're not doing the work that God is calling us to do. I needed to open myself to God's hand on my life. So I looked for projects with a larger purpose behind them. When *Jumping the Broom* came along, I said, "There's something about this film. I'm going to do what I can to get it made." I didn't worry about the small budget. I approached the opportunity from a place of faith and obedience to God. I had no idea that God would ultimately use the film to set up and prepare me for my life with Meagan.

Do you ever find yourself making bad relationship choices, even though you know better? What can you do to open yourself to God's hand in your life?

Holy Father, please use this day and the choices I make in it to prepare me for the future You have planned for me. Amen.

....
....
....
....
....
....
....
....
....

YOU ARE WHO YOU HANG WITH

If there is any consolation of love, if there is any fellowship
of the Spirit, if any affection and compassion, make my
joy complete by being of the same mind, maintaining the
same love, united in spirit, intent on one purpose.
—*Philippians 2:1–2 NASB*

Like it or not, you are who you hang with, and that's especially true when you're defying cultural norms. When you decide that you're going to be the one person in your circle who doesn't chase sex like dogs chase cars, you'll be pressured to conform. Most people are acutely aware of their harmful behavior patterns and dependence on instant gratification; however, to make themselves feel better, they'll try to get you to do the same. It's easier to resist that pressure when you're not doing it alone.

Our marriage is proof that God can and will bring like-minded people together. We both chose to opt out of the pursuit of dating traps that had failed us in the past in favor of the pursuit of wholeness, and when it was time and we were ready, God brought us together.

Like attracts like; it's a law of human nature. If you stay constant in your determination to do things the right way, you'll be surprised by how God will bring the right, healthy people into your life. And who knows—one of those people might be just the person you were meant to be with.

Are there people in your life who are sabotaging your practice of The Wait? What can you do to bring people into your life who will instead encourage you to stand strong?

Lord, please fill my life with people who will bless me and encourage me as I try to live Your way. Amen.

....

....

....

....

....

....

....

....

....

....

....

....

....

....

....

WHAT WAITING DOES, PART 1

Let's not get tired of doing what is good. At just the right time we will reap a harvest of blessing if we don't give up.
—*Galatians 6:9* NLT

Choosing The Wait allows you to retake control of your future. And it has benefits that affect all areas of your life, not just your dating and sexual relationships. For example:

- *Waiting reduces your risks*. Premarital sex can lead to some nasty outcomes, from sexually transmitted infections to babies you're not ready for. Abstaining reduces that risk to approximately zero.

- *Waiting reveals who your friends are*. Your real friends, the ones who want the best for you, will get behind The Wait and support you through it. False friends will ridicule you at best, and try to sabotage you at worst.

- *Waiting reveals your "triggers."* Triggers are people or situations that weaken your commitment to The Wait. They whisper things like, "Hurry, all your best friends are married." The Wait identifies your triggers and empowers you to resist them.

- *Waiting helps you think clearly*. Sex clouds judgment. But when you're seeking God and you're focused on whatever you're supposed to be doing, you see yourself and the other person clearly.

- *Waiting honors God's timing and methods*. God's hand bringing people into your life under the right circumstances at the right time helps strengthen your relationship with each other and the Lord.

- *Waiting helps you choose people because you like them and feel a connection with them*. Without sex as a go-to, you'll walk right past people who aren't right for you and choose to spend time with people whose character, intelligence, wit, and love for God you find irresistible.

Have you already seen benefits to practicing The Wait? What are they?

Lord, open my eyes to see the blessings that come from waiting for Your will to be done. Amen.

....

....

....

....

....

WHAT WAITING DOES, PART 2

My dear brothers and sisters, stand strong.
Do not let anything move you. Always give yourselves
fully to the work of the Lord, because you know
that your work in the Lord is never wasted.
—*1 Corinthians 15:58 NCV*

Practicing The Wait also . . .

- *Reduces drama, conflict, and expense*. How much cash and mental energy do we burn with the sole purpose of getting someone into bed? Then there's the post-sex morning-after scenes, waiting for the call that doesn't come, and feelings of being used. Giving up sex spares you all this.

- *Gives you better knowledge of your partner*. When you're not blinded by the counterfeit intimacy of premarital sex, you can see the person you're dating for who he or she really is.

- *Leads to better self-esteem*. If your significant other is with you only because of the sex, you might do some desperate things to keep him or her interested. Waiting lets you know that your partner is with you for you.

- *Will help bring clarity to engagement.* With sex on the sidelines, we were able to turn all our attention to the big questions. Did we share the same love of God? Were our tastes, interests, goals, and intellects compatible? When we decided that each answer was yes, we got engaged. With sex clouding the issues, getting to a proposal could take years.

- *Will help you choose God's plan A.* The Wait gives you space and time to discover who you are and who you can become, without the mad rush of chasing sex.

Instead of resenting your wait for the love of your life, decide to fulfill the potential God has placed in you. There's nothing disempowering about becoming God's collaborator in properly matching yourself with the life you deeply desire.

Think about the questions you want to be able to say yes to when you find the love of your life—questions about God, family, values, and careers. Now answer those questions for yourself. Are you the person you want to be?

Lord, teach me to work with You—and not against You—in the choices I make. Amen.

HOW WAITING GETS YOU
WHAT YOU WANT

*Therefore I urge you who have been chosen by God
to live up to the life to which God called you.*
—Ephesians 4:1 NCV

At first The Wait might seem uncomfortable, even lonely. But as you progress, your comfort grows. You start to see yourself not in the context of dating, sex, men, or other women, but as you. Then you start to see yourself as God sees you: a powerful source of love, life, healing, and so much more. You can control your sexuality. You can have a thriving career and a happy personal life. You can be brilliant, gorgeous, and assertive without apology. You do deserve the life that God's had waiting for you all this time.

When you wait, things become clear. You can tune out distractions and ask the kind of perception-sharpening questions you should have been asking all along:

- What have I been spending my energy and attention on and why?

- What have I been compromising to do that?

- Is what I'm doing filling me up or emptying me out?

- What is the driving force in my choices?

- What am I ready to sacrifice in order to change things and become my best self?

They're not easy questions to answer, especially if you've been hiding sick self-esteem or lifelong wounds underneath the disguise of a flirty serial dater. But if you have the courage to face the answers (and you do), they'll tell you something profound: living fully is not about needing a man to complete you. It's about wanting a man to partner with, to walk alongside the incredible woman you're becoming . . . the woman you're destined to be.

> It's time to be brave. Gather your courage, your honesty, and your journal and pen, and answer those questions.

Lord, I know that some things in my life need to change. Show me those things and help me to have the courage to change them. Amen.

....

....

....

....

....

....

....

ATTENTION AND CONTROL

Set your hearts on things above, where Christ is,
seated at the right hand of God. Set your minds
on things above, not on earthly things.
—*Colossians 3:1–3* NIV

Men desire as much control over their world and their place in it as possible. The tool to gain control is attention—where you focus your will. But you have only so much attention to spend. The more you spend on pursuits like casual sex, the less you have to "buy" the outcomes you really want. The Wait allows you to spend your attention wisely.

But can real men wait? Absolutely. How to begin? Take advantage of a natural male trait: a taste for dramatic jumps into the unknown. Take women completely out of the picture for a while. Delete the Black Book app from your phone. Too much? Okay, then start with being celibate for one week and see how it goes. Then add one more week. Use prayer to keep you centered. Practice self-control and discipline by working out and engaging in other things you enjoy. Most important, do a personal inventory built around these five key questions:

- What have I been spending my energy and attention on and why?

- What have I been compromising to do that?
- Is what I'm doing filling me up or emptying me out?
- What is the driving force in my choices?
- What am I ready to sacrifice in order to change things and become my best self?

Yes, you'll have to sacrifice plenty in order to wait. But you'll be amazed by the benefits—less stress and more peace and focus. Every child of God has an innate desire to do more and be more. So get to it, man.

Are you ready to get the things you really want out of this life God has given you? Then start by taking some time to answer—openly and honestly answer—the questions above.

Lord God, You are mighty and amazing, and You have created me to be mighty and amazing through You. Show me the way to do that. Amen.

TRIGGERS: EVERYONE HAS THEM

The temptations in your life are no different from what others experience. And God is faithful. He will not allow the temptation to be more than you can stand. When you are tempted, he will show you a way out so that you can endure.
—*1 Corinthians 10:13 NLT*

A trigger is anything that flips the panic switch in your brain and drives you to make reckless decisions. Knowing your triggers can help you either avoid them or learn to overcome the impulses that they provoke.

These are common triggers that seem to push most of us into bad relationships at one time or another:

- A friend or family member getting married

- Hitting an important birthday—turning thirty, for example

- A bad breakup

- The death of someone you know, especially someone close to you in age

- A life crisis such as divorce or job loss

- A crisis in your faith, such as doubting that God exists or has a plan for you

How many of these have you experienced? Did they trigger hasty or imprudent actions that you regretted later? Identifying your personal triggers is the first step toward disarming them. Start writing down the specific events, people, or circumstances that act as triggers for you. The clearer you are about them, the less they'll control you.

What are your personal triggers? Write them down, and share them with an accountability partner—someone who will help you disarm them.

Lord, You know the things that tempt me. I pray that You would shield me from them. And for those that do come my way, I pray that You would bless me with the strength to resist them. Amen.

....

....

....

....

....

....

....

....

....

WHAT WAS I THINKING?

Wise people think before they act; fools don't—
and even brag about their foolishness.
—*Proverbs 13:16* NLT

Sex is a topic overflowing with religious, cultural, political, and personal baggage. Much of our popular culture is built around sexual titillation. In our own business, the making of movies and television, actors are often cast as much for their good looks as for their acting talents. (You don't really think that all private detectives look like Denzel Washington, do you?)

As a people, we're alternately conflicted, fascinated, and appalled by sex in all its forms. Lawmakers crusade against pornography while their constituents consume it in record amounts. Abstinence-only sex-education programs deny teens basic information on the assumption that it will make them promiscuous, while the data show that teens are less sexually active than they've been in decades. The most popular magazines seem to be about nothing *but* sex: how to get it, how to give it, where to have it, how to be better at it, how to know if your partner is having it with someone else, and so on. We're obsessed with sex, and at the same time we disapprove of our obsession. It's no wonder that sex ties us in knots.

An old saying goes, "Success makes us forgetful and stupid." Sex does the same thing. It makes us forget who we are and what we want. It makes us do things that we look at later and say, "What was I thinking?"

Consider the culture around you. What is its attitude about sex? Does it honor God, or does it "brag about its foolishness"? Does it honor you—or the one you hope will one day be your spouse?

Lord, so many times I do things and then end up saying, "What was I thinking?" Before I act, help me to ask, "What do you think, Lord?" Amen.

....

....

....

....

....

....

....

....

....

....

....

....

THE TRAINING SEQUENCE

*I have fought the good fight, I have finished
the race, I have kept the faith.*
—2 Timothy 4:7 NIV

I f you think of your life as a fight movie, then The Wait
is like the training sequence. It's when the heroes train
harder than they ever have before. They use discipline,
hard work, and perseverance to prepare them for the fight
of their lives. In the movie of your life, think of your training methods as

- prayer
- meditation
- working out
- eating right
- studying
- growing
- creating
- seeking healthy relationships
- healing from negative relationships

These training methods will help you become the hero
you're destined to be. During this period of time, do what-

ever you need to do to fulfill the great potential that God has placed in you.

You might feel like you're already making steady progress toward becoming that person but could use a boost to get to the next level. On the other hand, maybe you're sick of being heartbroken and disappointed when it appears as if everything good in your life turns out to be a disappointment. Don't give up. Fight the good fight. There's nothing passive about this process. Quite the opposite, in fact. We can't think of a better strategy for getting what your heart desires than to become the kind of man or woman whose character attracts terrific people and whose skills and wisdom are the equal of any opportunity.

Are you honestly fighting the good fight? Is there one (or more than one) area of training that you need to focus more of your attention on? Plan now how you will do just that—then do it.

Lord, I realize that I am in training for the life You have laid out for me. Show me the areas I need to work on, and then help me to do it. Amen.

....

....

....

....

WHAT'S RIGHT VERSUS WHAT FEELS GOOD

Walk by the Spirit, and you will not
gratify the desires of the flesh.
—Galatians 5:16 ESV

There's no magic to The Wait. You just have to make the commitment and stick to it. First, acknowledge the power of your sex drive and that it's okay. You want sex. You want it a lot. You think about it. You fantasize. We all do. It's fine. There's nothing wrong or sinful about that. But you've got some questions you need to consider.

- What are you compromising to have sex?

- What is sex costing you?

- What are you not experiencing in your life that you might find if you stop obeying your sex drive and start obeying the Lord?

Once you've answered those questions, there's a still more important one to answer:

- Can you make doing what's right more important than doing what feels good?

For us, we were both able to be celibate independently because we arrived at a mental and spiritual place where following the Word and allowing God to work in our lives was more important than any short-term pleasure. If you're not at that point yet, it's better to admit that you're not ready for The Wait. Just know that if you keep living the way you've been living, you'll keep getting the same results. You'll know when you've had enough and are ready to try it. But if you are at that point, then you're ready for The Wait.

Take some time to answer that key question: *Can you make doing what's right more important than doing what feels good?* Does your life reflect your answer?

Lord, teach me to walk in Your ways, not the ways of this world or the ways of my own desires. Amen.

....
....
....
....
....
....
....
....
....

TELLING YOUR DATE ABOUT THE WAIT

You know that when your faith is tested, your endurance has a chance to grow. So let it grow, for when your endurance is fully developed, you will be perfect and complete, needing nothing.
—James 1:3–4 NLT

Once you make the decision to practice The Wait, there's one issue you'll have to deal with sooner or later: telling potential partners about your wait.

It's wise to prepare for people's reactions when you tell them that you're celibate, because the hard truth is that some will want nothing to do with it. That's a sacrifice you must be willing to make. In the long run, bypassing relationships with people who don't want the same things you want out of life is a blessing. When we started dating, it was a blessing that we were both celibate, but that's rare. More likely, you'll meet someone fascinating, and before too much time passes you'll tell him or her that you're celibate. Be clear about your motives: your love of God and your desire to be a better person and have a better life. Some people will laugh. Some will get angry. It will be obvious when you find a person who shares your values and goals.

But what if you've come to The Wait because someone

you like asked you to forgo sex? Does it mean as much as it does when it's your idea?

Of course it does. You're still making the choice to wait. You're saying, "I like this person and I'm going to do whatever it takes to be with him/her." Any path into The Wait is a good one if it brings you to the destiny God has in mind for you.

> Take a little time to practice how you will broach the subject of The Wait with your next date. Prepare for both types of reactions—positive and negative.

Lord, as I share my decision to wait with others, help me to remember why I am waiting and bless me with the words to explain those reasons. Amen.

....
....
....
....
....
....
....
....
....
....

LET GOD BE THE MATCHMAKER

For God is working in you, giving you the desire
and the power to do what pleases him.
—Philippians 2:13 NLT

God is always at the heart of The Wait. But in trying to force the action in your life, you can easily overlook the fact that you're not the matchmaker of your life. God is. God has a way of matching us with opportunities that align with His divine plan. He already has the right life and relationship in mind for you. It may not be with the type of person you have in mind, and it may not be under the circumstances that you think are most desirable. But God knows how to make the perfect match if we allow Him to match us.

The catch to this matchmaking is free will. We can ignore God's intentions for our lives; many people do. He's not going to force us to live according to His will. However, God will put signs in our path—people, events, opportunities—that can show us the path that leads to joy and fulfillment. Then it's up to us to decide if we want to humble ourselves and submit to His plan, even if it seems to lead us away from what we want most.

If you've failed to choose God's will for your life, even multiple times, you know what? There's nothing wrong with you. That just means you're human. All the relationship failures, bouts of loneliness, and romantic twists straight out of a romance novel . . . God can use all that to match you with the right person and the life He's always wanted you to have.

> Are you allowing God to be at the heart of your wait? Are you allowing Him to reveal His plan to you, or are you still trying to dictate your plan to Him?

Lord, I pray that You will help me to completely surrender my life and my search for the right person to You and to Your perfect plan. Amen.

GIVING UP THE ILLUSION

This is the confidence we have in approaching God: that
if we ask anything according to his will, he hears us.
—1 John 5:14 NIV

Let's be honest: most of us aren't interested in being patient. What we really want is to find our perfect soul mate *right now*. If we happen to be patient, it's because there are no other options. Meanwhile, we work hard to assemble a great life that leaves nothing to chance:

- Move to a city that's good for singles? *Check.*
- Work out and get fit? *Check.*
- Make sure what we wear, drive, and eat all make us look like a great catch? *Triple check.*

We're going to climb the mountain, get the promotion, and make a lot of money. Then, like in a film where the director just shouted "Action!" our perfect life partner will walk through the door. Yes, you should make yourself as desirable as possible and put yourself in the position to meet quality single people. But problems begin when you believe you can order a life partner the way you order a pizza: "I'd like a man who loves the Lord, six foot two, with brown eyes." Or, "I'd like a bad girl shaped like an hourglass, intelligent, and with great feet."

The Bible does say, "Ask, and ye shall receive" (John 16:24, KJV). The danger comes when we think God isn't listening unless He brings us a mate who's exactly to our specifications. What if God is bringing someone into your life who will fulfill every need, but who is very different from your physical ideal? If you're only looking for the ideal, you can miss out.

> What characterizes your ideal soul mate? How many of those characteristics are physical, as opposed to spiritual or emotional? Do you see how physical ideals could blind you to that special person God has for you?

Lord, I am asking You to bring the perfect person for me into my life—and I am also asking that You open my eyes and my heart to recognize that person. Amen.

....

....

....

....

....

....

"THE ONE"

"I know what I am planning for you," says the
LORD. *"I have good plans for you, not plans to hurt*
you. I will give you hope and a good future."
—Jeremiah 29:11 NCV

When we start talking about God's will, some people leap to the idea of "the One," and that can be
problematic. It's a deeply romantic notion that there's one
perfect person for you somewhere in the world, and you're
drawing inexorably closer to each other.

Of course, finding the right one usually isn't that easy.
When you don't meet "the One" by your self-imposed
deadline, it's easy to surrender to panic, discard God's plan,
and engage in desperate, reckless behavior to bring love
into your life at any cost. Then you're back to the quick
fix: jump into a stranger's bed or do something foolish like
rushing into a marriage without God's blessing. Inevitably,
things fall apart and you're on the side of the road,
wounded, surveying the wreckage and wondering what
happened.

Let's be clear. The Wait is not some genie-in-the-bottle
practice that will make your perfect person magically appear. First of all, in God's perfect plan there is one person
who is right for each of us and who has been called to mar-

riage. If both people follow God's will, they will find each other. But some don't. Some people put their will before the Lord's. Does that mean you're meant to be single for the rest of your life?

No, God always has a contingency plan. He's made us compatible with many different types of people. God will provide a way for you to meet someone else who is the right match for you—someone who will bring you joy, happiness, and peace.

Be honest: are you expecting The Wait to make "the One" magically appear? Why is this not a good idea?

Holy Lord, I know You have a plan for my life. Help me to surrender to that plan—even if it's different from what I think the plan should be. Amen.

....

....

....

....

....

....

....

....

....

THE REALITY OF THE SOUL MATE

*May you experience the love of Christ, though it is too great
to understand fully. Then you will be made complete with
all the fullness of life and power that comes from God.*
—*Ephesians 3:19* NLT

Do you remember the "you complete me" line from *Jerry Maguire*? True, Tom Cruise's character says the line in the movie, but the idea—that we need a soul mate to complete us and make us whole—is troubling. Because the reality most women face is very different.

When God created you, He made you a whole woman, a child of the Lord with everything you need to grow into a source of love, light, and power in this world. So why do most women believe the truest form of happiness can be achieved only once they find Mr. Right?

It's because while God created you as a complete being unto yourself, He also created man to be your partner, the one who brings out the very best of you. That's not the same as needing a man to complete you. God intends for us to bring out the best versions of each other. Your husband is your partner in purpose. And the two of you are supposed to hold each other accountable, be each other's cheerleader, and help each other accomplish your individual and collective purposes.

The thing is, you can't just go out and find that man. He also has to find you, and that won't happen until you're ready. As a woman, it's your responsibility to work on developing the fullness of who God created you to be before you give yourself to your husband. Until you do that, you won't be ready to find and keep that perfect partner. God, not man, completes you.

Are you looking for a man to complete you? Why isn't that a good, or even godly, idea? What are you doing to fully realize who you are in God?

Lord God, You are the One—the only One—who truly completes me. Help me to find myself in You. Amen.

THE REALITY OF THE LIST

Be sure that no one leads you away with false and empty teaching that is only human, which comes from the ruling spirits of this world, and not from Christ. All of God lives fully in Christ (even when Christ was on earth), and you have a full and true life in Christ.
—*Colossians 2:8–10 NCV*

For guys, self-worth is based on what other guys think. So if you decide to challenge the male status quo, you will be met with resistance from other men who think waiting makes men less masculine. The thinking goes like this: the more conquests you have, the more validation you get, and the better you feel. With this ethos permeating every part of male culture, celibacy isn't just inconceivable. It's perceived as insane. Then we add to that the obstacle of the List.

The List is that unspoken inventory of must-haves that plays on a 24/7 loop in the minds of many men. It contains every seductive, delirious worldly goal you can think of:

- Wealth

- Power

- Position

- A hot car

- Great clothes

- A huge crib

- Big toys

- A beautiful, sexy woman on your arm

It's all bling, and men easily lose themselves in the conquest and competition. But the problem with the List is that the rewards are transactional—that is, to get something, you have to give up something you won't get back. For a lot of men, that something is time with their families, their peace of mind, or their very character.

God made men aggressive, competitive, sexual beings, but He also made them capable of more. The List is a placebo. Because real success isn't just professional or sexual, but moral, personal, and spiritual. The List is a lie. It won't make a man more of a man. But The Wait will.

What's on your List? Is it filled with only the things of this world? Or does it contain moral, personal, and spiritual items, as well? What would God think of your List?

Lord, change me from the inside out. Make my List look more and more like Your List every day. Amen.

THE CHALLENGES OF CELIBACY

Since we are living by the Spirit, let us follow the Spirit's leading in every part of our lives.
—*Galatians 5:25* NLT

The choice to become celibate comes at one of four stages, depending on where you are in your dating life, and each comes with its own challenges.

- *The first stage is celibacy while you're dating around.* At this stage, celibacy is easier. You're not overly attached to anybody. Keep reminding yourself of your goals: to meet lots of people, let God work in your spirit, and break problematic patterns.

- *The second stage is celibacy when you're dating exclusively.* You're spending a lot of time together and the chemistry is strong. Communication is critical. It's up to you both to keep each other strong and committed.

- *The third stage is being celibate in a committed relationship.* You can see the finish line—marriage—from where you're standing. But you might find yourself thinking, "It's so close, why not just give in? We'll probably get married anyway." This is when it's incredibly important to look into the future and imagine the possible outcomes to that choice. Avoid mistakes by being honest about what might happen.

- *The fourth stage is when you're already in a committed relationship and having sex*. Spiritually, you might want to stop and practice The Wait because you feel this is what God wants from you. Practically, you might want to gain more clarity of mind to see if this person is truly your spouse. Because you're already in an established pattern of sexual behavior, this is probably the hardest of all stages. But it can be done.

Regardless of the stage you are in, The Wait empowers you to make choices that are more likely to bring you into the fullness of God's best destiny for you.

What stage of The Wait are you in? What are the particular challenges you are facing at this time? Take some time to create a tangible, practical plan for dealing with those challenges.

Lord, you know the struggles and the temptations I face. Help me to conquer them this day and each day, until You bring that special someone into my life. Amen.

BE PREPARED

Control yourselves and be careful! The devil, your enemy,
goes around like a roaring lion looking for someone to eat.
Refuse to give in to him, by standing strong in your faith.
—*1 Peter 5:8–9* NCV

We're living, married proof that you can resist temptation and remain celibate even when you're in a committed, marriage-minded relationship with someone you're madly in love with. You can do the same, but not if you don't plan and prepare. You have to accept that temptation is coming for you. Not only that, but unless you live in a monastery, temptation is going to be hanging out pretty much 24/7. You've got to have strategies for dealing with it—for bolstering your will when you're weak, for avoiding the triggers that set off your desire, and for getting the heck out of the room when resistance is futile.

- How will you handle it when dates offer to take you out somewhere that you know might weaken your commitment?

- What will you do when you're close with someone who's clearly ready to get it on with you?

- How can you change your physical environment to manage things that will get you thinking, fantasizing, and obsessing about sex?

You've got to be prepared. The Wait isn't for people who think their willpower is so strong they don't need to think and plan. Nobody's willpower is bulletproof. If you've already had sex and are used to getting it, going without it will feel unnatural at first. You can't wing this. If you're going to make a promise to yourself and God, do everything in your power to keep it.

Take some time to address the situations above. Develop a strategy, and share it with a friend who will hold you accountable.

Holy Lord, please fill me with the wisdom to know how to stand strong against temptation—and the determination to actually do it. Amen.

IT GETS EASIER

Don't copy the behavior and customs of this world, but
let God transform you into a new person by changing
the way you think. Then you will learn to know God's
will for you, which is good and pleasing and perfect.
—*Romans 12:2* NLT

Living without sex does get easier, especially when you're not in a committed, serious relationship. Initially, yeah, it's rough. You're not giving your body what it wants, and like a chocolate lover craving some 70 percent cacao, you're thinking about it all the time. Then some time passes and it gets better. Your mind gains control.

Sex can become a pleasurable addiction, and like any addiction it takes time to break free. It will happen. In Gary Keller's book *The ONE Thing*, he says that it takes sixty-six days to create a new habit. We love applying that idea to The Wait. Sixty-six days of no sex will put you on the path you need to achieve what you want—and what God wants for you. You'll love the clarity, the power, and the feeling of being in control. And you'll love the blessings it brings into your life.

As your time of waiting lengthens, does it seem to be getting easier for you? Are there specific practices that make it easier? How can you increase those practices?

Holy Lord, use this time of waiting to bring clarity to my life and to my role in Your kingdom. Amen.

*The Lord is faithful, and he will strengthen
you and protect you from the evil one.*
—2 Thessalonians 3:3 NIV

I f your faith is strong, the hunger to be better and do more can be reason enough to keep you committed to celibacy. It's simply not worth it to fail. The possibility that we might miss out on what God had in store for us was a big part of what kept us on track.

Reminding yourself of your goal to grow into God's purpose can help you remain committed. Here's a prayer that will help you overcome temptation:

The Lust Prayer

God, please help me get control over this beast called Lust. I will not let it destroy me or disrupt the destiny You have set for my life. You said You would provide a way of escape when temptation appears, so show me the exit sign right now, Lord, because I'm about to do something that will please my flesh but harm my spirit. I'm tired of continuously falling prey to lust. Give me the victory today! I claim authority over my body, my heart, my mind, and my sexuality. You made me sexual but give me the tools to manage this sexuality in a way that pleases You! You said

You'd never leave nor forsake me, so I'm trusting in you, Lord. You have authority over this lust and I claim that authority now. Be my strength when I am weak and deliver me from this flesh that threatens to destroy every good thing You've planned for my life. I pray this prayer in the mighty name of Jesus, Amen!

Write out your own prayer for dealing with the temptation in your life today.

Lord, I know You will never leave me to face this battle alone. Strengthen me to fight this fight. Amen.

....

....

....

....

....

....

....

....

....

....

....

....

THE WAIT AND ... CREATIVITY

God created mankind in his own image, in the image of
God he created them; male and female he created them.
—*Genesis 1:27* NIV

Everyone has a creative spark; it's part of our legacy from God, the Creator. We're all creators in one way or another. But for those of us dying to find that creative spark and create something great—a script, a play, a poem, a painting, a monologue—finding our creative voice can be torture. We live in a city and work in an industry where everyone is trying to act, write or produce a screenplay, become a director, or do something else creative, so we know what frustrated creativity looks like.

The trouble is that we want to create ... *now*. But nothing suppresses inspiration like having to be creative on demand. The creative mind isn't Netflix. You can't press a button and order an idea for a movie or a great melody for a song. You have to wait.

The core principles of The Wait apply beautifully to creative people: quieting the mind, listening to the inner voice, letting go of trying to make things happen, doing other things to distract from the need to have results now. When you do these things, you free your subconscious, where genius lives. That's when you can create miracles.

In what area does your creative side show through? What frees you up to be creative—time alone, music, nature?

Lord, You are the Master of Creativity, and You have instilled Your creativity within me. Show me how to best use it to please and to delight You. Amen.

....
....
....
....
....
....
....
....
....
....
....
....
....
....
....
....
....

KNOW YOURSELF

"Lead us not into temptation."
—*Matthew 6:13 KJV*

The most powerful tool for staying disciplined and keeping your commitment is your faith in and love of God. If you keep in mind that you're doing this as an act of obedience and to receive the fullness of what God has in store for you, you'll have an easier time avoiding sexual temptation.

It's just as important that you take responsibility for yourself. Some people say, "Well, things just happen." That's a cop-out. We let things happen if we're okay with them, even if we won't admit it to ourselves.

Even if your faith has weak moments (which we all have), the most effective way to be successful in your commitment to celibacy is to know your triggers. Avoid setting yourself up for failure. It's not the act of sex that's the problem, but the moments leading up to it. You can't stand next to the tracks and then pretend you're not trying to catch a train.

So don't just rely on loving the Lord and being strong. Know yourself. If going inside your date's house is likely to lead to serious kissing and possibly other things, say good night at the door. If staying at someone's house after midnight is dangerous for your willpower, agree in advance to part ways at eleven thirty. If kissing leads down the slippery slope, stop at a hug.

Your spirit should be telling your body what to do, not the other way around. Know your limits, monitor yourself, and communicate. Remember, you are in this for the long run, not a quick sprint.

Are you ever tempted to say, "Well, things just happen," when you've made a mistake? Be honest: are you standing next to the tracks, pretending you're not trying to catch a train?

Lord, I want to take responsibility for my weaknesses. Help me to acknowledge my triggers and then give me the determination and strength to avoid them. Amen.

....

....

....

....

....

....

....

....

....

BUT YOU'RE MISERABLE

*For the LORD God is our sun and our shield. He
gives us grace and glory. The LORD will withhold no
good thing from those who do what is right.*
—Psalm 84:11 NLT

So you've embraced the idea of The Wait. You've seen the light: getting your head clear and getting your life in order so God can bless you means, first, giving up sex. Good for you.

Too bad you're miserable, right?

Maybe that's overstating it, but you're thinking about sex a lot, aren't you? You're trying to be strong, but your body is craving sexual satisfaction. Curtailing the drive to call that "friend with benefits" or hook up with an ex is tough. You know this is the right thing, but . . . temptation is everywhere.

Believe it, we feel you. We fought the natural desire for more than a year from the time we started dating to the time we married. Some days were easier than others, but staying celibate was never easy. Sometimes the sexual chemistry was so hot that we simply couldn't be in the same room together. That's okay; sometimes wisdom means seeing that a situation has the potential to pack some serious sexual tension and changing your plans. It means knowing that when you wear that dress and he wears that suit you can't keep your hands off each other, so you wear something else.

It would have been so simple to play the "just this once" game. But we didn't. We wanted to see if we could do what others deemed impossible. We wanted to see if there really was something to be gained by waiting. And there definitely was.

> Is The Wait proving to be a huge struggle for you? When is it easier? More difficult?

Lord, You are stronger than any temptation I'll ever face. Help me to rely on Your strength to keep me committed to The Wait. Amen.

....
....
....
....
....
....
....
....
....
....

WHAT TEMPTATION LOOKS LIKE

"Keep watch and pray, so that you will not give in to temptation. For the spirit is willing, but the body is weak!"
—*Matthew 26:41* NLT

How are you likely to be tempted to break your celibacy pledge? Some scenarios seem obvious: the second-date make-out session that becomes a little too hot and heavy; the beautiful person you just met who invites you to come in after you've had one drink too many. But honestly, how often does that sort of thing really happen? Genuine temptation, we've found, is more insidious. It doesn't seem like you're in trouble until you're more than halfway there. That's when you have to be careful.

Sexual temptation sneaks up on you and catches you when you're weak—which, let's face it, is pretty much whenever you're breathing and awake. Temptation will fit anywhere in your life that you make room for it: work flirtations, having contact with exes, pornography, you name it. In practicing The Wait, one of your goals is to create a lifestyle that acknowledges temptation by putting as many safeguards as possible in place.

That's a lot easier when you can custom-fit your anti-temptation plan to your circumstances and triggers. For example, the desire for sex when you're off the dating scene is very different from when you're in a serious relationship.

Figure out your triggers, remember your commitment to God and why you're waiting, and create a plan that addresses the temptation you face.

Are you making room for temptation in your life? Take an honest look at your life—from your social media to your contacts list to your hangout habits. What do you need to clean up?

Lord, show me the areas where I am allowing—even welcoming—temptation into my life. And then help me to get rid of them. Amen.

TAME YOUR TRIGGERS

Give yourselves completely to God. Stand against
the devil, and the devil will run from you.
—James 4:7 NCV

Each of us has our own personal triggers, those things that just naturally set our blood to boiling. But here are some major—and pretty universal—triggers to be mindful of:

- *Late nights.* Movie night on the couch in somebody's apartment is fun, but it can lead to more.

- *Emotional trauma.* When you get in a fight with someone, get in trouble at work, or just feel bad, you're vulnerable and want comfort. Be careful.

- *Intimate contact.* Be affectionate, but be mindful if that affection is making it difficult for you or the person you're dating to resist temptation. If it is, dial down the intensity.

- *Alcohol.* Drinking and celibacy probably isn't the best mix. Liquor reduces your inhibitions and makes you more likely to do something you'll regret. If you're waiting, consider doing it sober. Either that or make the choice not to drink (or drink minimally) around the person you're dating.

- *Sexting and Snapchat.* Provocative texts or video clips can send you over the edge if your willpower is wavering.

- *Travel.* Hookups on the road can seem like they don't count, kind of like calories from ice cream that you eat when nobody's watching. What? Of course, sex when you're on the road counts. Don't fool yourself.

What are your personal triggers? What strategies have you found that help you avoid them? What strategies haven't worked?

Lord, teach me to use the wisdom and the knowledge You've given me to stay strong in my commitment to The Wait. Amen.

....

....

....

....

....

....

....

WISE WAITING AND ... ALCOHOL

*"Watch out! Don't let your hearts be dulled by carousing
and drunkenness, and by the worries of this life."*
—*Luke 21:34* NLT

Celibacy is all about keeping a cool, clear head while you're getting to know someone, and to that end, we suggest that if you drink, go easy on the alcohol during those early dates. We live in a hookup culture, and alcohol is the social lubricant that we use to have fun. But all too often, two people have a few too many drinks and wind up in bed together. That's a great way to find yourself linked to someone you don't even know—and an even better way to end up with a disease or a child.

Monitoring and limiting your drinking, especially during early dates when you're just learning about that person, keeps your head clear and perceptions sharp. It also allows you to present yourself honestly. If you become reckless or the life of the party after a few drinks, you might put yourself in danger and impair your judgment, which is key to successful dating.

Since celibacy is all about keeping a "cool, clear head," why does that make alcohol an unwise, dangerous addition to a date? If this is something you struggle with, develop some strategies to limit your alcohol intake, such as double-dating with an accountability partner.

Dear Lord, help me to turn away from anything that would lead me into greater temptation. Amen.

....

....

....

....

....

....

....

....

....

....

....

....

....

....

....

....

USE WHATEVER WORKS

Run from sexual sin! No other sin so clearly
affects the body as this one does. For sexual
immorality is a sin against your own body.
—1 Corinthians 6:18 NLT

From technology to dating tactics, anything that helps you stay disciplined is fair game. Some suggestions:

- *Put technology to work for you.* Set a "go home" alarm on your smartphone. Ask a friend to send you an "Are you guys being good?" text message at a preset time.

- *Avoid people who talk about sex all the time.* Some people just can't help talking about sex—their own sexual exploits, sex on TV and in film, and so on. If you're feeling weak, ask such people to change the conversation.

- *Double-date or date in social groups.* Going out with a group reduces the pressure that sometimes comes with a one-on-one date.

- *Control your environment.* Some places are inherently charged with sexual energy: nightclubs, strip clubs, and the like. And sometimes, it's not the location but the situation, like a late-night work session with an attractive colleague.

- *Stay away from graphic sexual imagery.* It's incredibly easy to find graphic sexuality, especially online, and it's become a daily habit for some. Break it. Clear your browser cache and delete any bookmarks to suggestive websites.

- *Stay busy.* An idle mind is the devil's playground. Find activities that allow you to use your energy in life-improving ways. Volunteer. Travel. Work on your house. Fill up your days so your focus is on what you're doing, not what you're *not* doing.

Use whatever works to keep you waiting and fulfilling your commitment, because nothing else will bring you more blessings.

Which of these suggestions would best help you stay committed to The Wait? Put it into practice today.

Lord, help me learn to turn away from the temptations of this world, instead of running to them. Amen.

....

....

THINKING LESS ABOUT SEX

Whatever is true, whatever is noble, whatever is right, whatever is pure, whatever is lovely, whatever is admirable—if anything is excellent or praiseworthy—think about such things.
—Philippians 4:8 NIV

Hamlet said, "There is nothing either good or bad, but thinking makes it so." When the subject is sex, truer words were never spoken. When we can't have something, we can't stop thinking about it. When that something is sex, the endless thoughts make it harder to stay committed and tempt us to chase empty gratification. The solution: stop thinking about sex so much. Yes, we know that's like an elephant sitting in the middle of a room while someone's telling you, "Don't think about the elephant!" But it can be done.

- Pray or meditate every day, multiple times a day. Both will help quiet anxiety and promote calm.

- If you know others who are practicing The Wait or who are celibate for other reasons, create a support group, even if it's a virtual one.

- Carry a meaningful object or token that reminds you of your commitment to God and to celibacy.

- Write down a statement of why you're choosing to wait and keep it in your phone. Reminding yourself of why you're waiting is key to keeping the commitment.

- Ask friends who keep sending you sexual material to stop.

Is it over the top to avoid friends who talk about sex, music that promotes it, or movies with lovemaking scenes? It all depends on your triggers. Figure out what gets you dwelling on those things that fuel your lust and take steps to avoid them. Remember, commitment is half willpower and half common sense.

> Think about Hamlet's line, "There is nothing either good or bad, but thinking makes it so." What does that mean to you? How does that meaning impact your thought life and your commitment to The Wait?

Lord, I know my thoughts control my actions, so please teach me to control my thoughts. Amen.

....

....

....

....

THE WAIT AS A DISCIPLINE: A MAN'S PERSPECTIVE

Prepare your minds for action and exercise self-control.
—*1 Peter 1:13* NLT

The Wait is a discipline. And because men and women are different, the way they approach the discipline of The Wait also differs.

Men tend to be sexually driven, so the methods to keep men in The Wait need to be fairly . . . extreme. For example:

- *Block the numbers of any women you've been seeing who you aren't serious about.* Make their contacting you a lost cause. Rude? Maybe. If you're concerned, text or email the women you really care about in the beginning and tell them what you're doing.

- *Have an accountability buddy*. That's someone you meet with regularly who doesn't let you backslide. It could be a friend, sibling, pastor, or colleague. But make sure it's someone you can talk to who won't let you off the hook.

- *Quit porn.* Yes, even Christian men have been known to look at pornography. Ethical issues aside, it's bad for the willpower. Set up your web browser to block it, and stop tempting yourself.

- *Get involved in something that challenges and improves you.* Join a networking group or basketball league. Hit the gym. Do something that enriches body, mind, and spirit—as well as improves your extracurricular time.

- *Build a stronger prayer life.* We can't stress this enough. Prayer will be your lifeline when you feel weak or when doubts torture your mind. Have a daily prayer practice.

- *Volunteer.* Commit to a church ministry; work with a nonprofit or with fatherless boys. This will focus you on gratitude and your own blessings.

How is The Wait a discipline? What is it in your life that needs to be more disciplined? Pick one of these actions and get started on it today.

Lord, help me to do what is needed to keep my commitment to You and to The Wait. Amen.

....

....

....

THE WAIT AS A DISCIPLINE: A WOMAN'S PERSPECTIVE

Whoever pursues righteousness and unfailing love
will find life, righteousness, and honor.
—*Proverbs 21:21* NLT

Like working out or eating low-carb, The Wait is a discipline. It's difficult to sustain a life without sex, possibly because it's counter to the way you've conducted your life up to now. That means it's important to have a set of disciplined practices that will keep you focused, positive, and gaining new strength over time. For women, these might include:

- Regular prayer (a must)
- Meditating: making time to reflect on areas of growth or needed growth
- Fasting
- Self-care, such as getting enough sleep
- Doing something positive to increase your self-confidence
- Journaling
- Talking with a pastor or spiritual mentor
- Getting counsel from other women who have successfully waited

- Growing your career
- Examining past relationship patterns
- Making peace with people from your past who hurt you or with whom you have unresolved conflict

Pick an item from the list above to focus on today. How will that focus help you remain committed to The Wait?

Lord, open my eyes to see who I am in You and Your purpose for me in Your kingdom. Let me be useful to You while I wait. Amen.

....
....
....
....
....
....
....
....
....
....
....
....

TEAR UP YOUR LIST

"The LORD doesn't see things the way you see them. People judge by outward appearance, but the LORD looks at the heart."
—1 Samuel 16:7 NLT

Tear up your List. You know what we're talking about. That checklist that details everything about the One: what that person will look like, how much money the person will make, what race he or she will be, everything that represents your ideal person down to hair color, eye color, height, weight, body type, occupation, personality, and more.

Here's the thing: we all know that nobody is going to check every box on that List. But we keep searching for someone who does! By looking for characteristics instead of people, we often prematurely accept or reject potential partners based on traits that might wind up being unimportant if we got to know them better as people.

A big part of The Wait is about breaking old patterns, and one of those patterns has to do with the type of person you've typically dated. The one who fits your List. Instead, try deliberately dating out of your usual type and see what happens. If you've always been attracted to tall guys, try dating shorter ones. If you've always been attracted to women with long hair, give one with short hair a shot.

What have you got to lose? The type you've been dating hasn't led to anything lasting, so try something new.

When you free yourself from being so rigidly attached to your List, you realize that once you find someone God has for you, someone you connect with on an emotional, intellectual, practical, and spiritual level, this is the foundation of real, unconditional love.

How attached are you to your List? Have you ever dated someone outside your List? Would you be open to it now?

Lord, help me to see others not according to some artificial checklist, but according to Your standards, according to their heart. Amen.

....

....

....

....

....

....

....

....

....

....

THE JURY-BOX MENTALITY

*Let the morning bring me word of your unfailing
love, for I have put my trust in you. Show me the
way I should go, for to you I entrust my life.*
—Psalm 143:8 NIV

Because it's so tempting to confuse the flush and rush of
a kiss with love, dating while waiting demands a fresh
approach to the social scene. You need to adopt what we
call the jury-box mentality.

Here's what we mean: On a jury, every time you leave
the courtroom the judge will instruct you not to draw any
conclusions about the case. You're not supposed to decide
innocence or guilt until all the evidence is in. You're ex-
pected to remain in a state of nonjudgment.

That's exactly the way you should be dating when
you're in The Wait. People really, really want to fall in
love. But infatuation clouds our reason and impairs our
ability to make good decisions. Falling for somebody
makes it harder to look at the person critically, see flaws,
and ask important questions like, "Do you want kids one
day?" or "How did your last relationship end?" How
often have you let yourself be so blinded by attraction that
you've ignored or excused a lover's serious transgressions,
only to kick yourself later? We've all done it.

Instead of letting yourself fall head over heels before you really know the other person, venture into the dating scene with a jury-box mentality, observing and learning but not judging. Don't commit to anyone prematurely. That doesn't mean you can't have fun. It means that you don't rush to judge someone as "the One" based on a few encounters, a few dates, or even a few church services together.

Think back over your past relationships. How would using the jury-box mentality have changed the outcome of those relationships?

Lord, You know this dating is like a minefield. Help me to keep my wits about me and to date with wisdom and discernment. Amen.

....

....

....

....

....

....

....

....

....

....

WHEN YOU MEET SOMEONE AMAZING

Be very careful, then, how you live—not as unwise but
as wise, making the most of every opportunity.
—*Ephesians 5:15–16* NIV

Being in The Wait does not mean you'll automatically know what to do when you meet someone amazing. In fact, meeting someone like that could make waiting harder! What do you do? Do you date this person? Do you wait for God to tell you what to do? We definitely come down on the side of getting out there and testing the waters—carefully. When in doubt, go out. But do it armed with some knowledge about this tricky thing called infatuation.

Infatuation (or sometimes what we think is love) can be an addictive substance. It's amazing to feel that rush of hormones and that electricity when you meet, touch, or kiss someone for the first time. Like songs and movies have said before us, infatuation is a drug.

Infatuation is defined as an intense but short-lived passion or admiration for someone. The problems start when we let the effects of infatuation, not our reason and character, dictate our actions. That's when we make reckless, foolish, self-destructive choices—over and over and over again. Sometimes you can get so infatuated with someone that you think it's real love, but instead of waiting to evaluate this you move too fast with that person. By the time infatuation wears off, you're in so deep, it's hard to get out.

Have you ever been caught up in an infatuation? What did that experience teach you? How does infatuation differ from love?

Lord, give me the wisdom to discern between infatuation and love—and the strength of character to remain true to my commitment. Amen.

....
....
....
....
....
....
....
....
....
....
....
....
....

ARE YOU AN INFATUATION ADDICT?

For the world offers only a craving for physical pleasure, a craving for everything we see, and pride in our achievements and possessions. These are not from the Father, but are from this world.
—*1 John 2:16* NLT

Bad daters are, essentially, infatuation addicts. Do you have a friend who's constantly repeating the same awful behavior with girls or guys? Everybody has at least one. (Hint: If you don't have one, odds are *you* are the one.) This person hurtles from one doomed relationship to another. Take a look at this pattern:

- Your friend cleans up the mess after a tormented, horrible breakup and swears never to make the same mistakes again.

- Your friend meets someone new and after an unnervingly short period, insists that it's love.

- You spot serious red flags, but when you mention them (and remind your friend about the pledge not to repeat past relationship blunders), he or she gets angry and insists this person is the One.

- The infatuation goes south: fights, lying, accusations, the whole horror show.

- The inevitable nasty breakup happens, leaving your friend shattered—and if this has been going on long enough, possibly straining your friendship.

Sound familiar? Most of us have done it at one time or another. Some do it for years before finally realizing they've been DUI: "Dating Under Infatuation." We're hooked by the jumpy shot of adrenaline when he touches our arm, the warm rush we feel when she smiles from across the room.

That's sweet and seductive, but it ain't love. Love is deeper, more mature, and subtler. When we confuse it with infatuation and sexual chemistry, we waste years chasing shadows and blinding ourselves to how God is trying to bless us.

Do you know anyone who is an infatuation addict? (Is it you?) How does chasing infatuation steal you of the opportunity to discover God's true blessings for your life?

Holy Lord, help me learn to look before I leap, to talk to You before I give my heart and my body away. Amen.

....

....

....

A POWERFUL RELATIONSHIP SECRET

*"Likewise, every good tree bears good fruit, but a
bad tree bears bad fruit. A good tree cannot bear bad
fruit, and a bad tree cannot bear good fruit."*
—Matthew 7:17–18 NIV

Waiting is about keeping a cool head, analyzing the situation, and staying rational. Despite the pressure and your desire to be in love and be loved, you're choosing to see how things play out before you make a decision about whether this person is or isn't right for you. This lets you in on an incredibly powerful relationship secret:

People will eventually reveal themselves if you allow them to.

Often, we conspire with people to keep them from showing us who they really are. We fall in love with an idea of who we want someone to be, but we don't allow time and space for that person to show us who he or she is.

In our industry, we've met some incredible actors, but we've discovered some of the greatest acting goes on in relationships. People play the part of the supportive boyfriend or caring girlfriend, but it's just an act. Trouble is, by the time we get the memo, we're so deep into the relationship that it's hard—even damaging—to back out.

By practicing The Wait, you'll hold on to your ability to see potential partners clearly—gifts, faults, and all. You'll slow things down. You won't commit too soon. You'll put your own needs first, which is exactly what you should do. And you'll retain the self-control to say good-bye to anyone who doesn't meet your standards, doesn't treat you with respect, or infects your life with his or her drama.

Have you ever fallen in love with the idea of who a person is, rather than the reality of who that person is? What steps can you take in future dating relationships to make sure that doesn't happen?

Lord, help me date with my eyes and ears wide open, to see people as they really are. And help me also to be honest about who I really am. Amen.

....

....

....

....

....

....

....

....

....

BUT YOU'RE BORED

Above all else, guard your heart, for
everything you do flows from it.
—Proverbs 4:23 NIV

You're practicing The Wait. You're celibate. You're working on yourself in body, mind, and spirit. But you're bored. You don't want to sit at home or spend all your time at the gym, at work, or at church. You want some fun. So you're asking questions. *Should I date right now? When is God going to bring the right person? When is someone going to ask me out? When am I going to meet "the One"?* These are the questions that plague you when you're single. Don't worry—they plagued us, too. Let's be honest: the longer these questions go unanswered, the more depressed we tend to become. How do we remain patient with the process yet active while we're waiting?

The answer is definitely not "don't date." You can date while you're practicing The Wait. You just can't date the way you did before. Remember that The Wait is not just about sex. The principles behind The Wait—productive patience, listening to God, working on perfecting yourself, and letting good things happen—will benefit you in all areas of your relationships and your life. Dating is a perfect example. Even if you're practicing The Wait, you still need to assess whether you and your partner have passion. You'll need passion for your marriage to be successful. Letting sex wait allows you to evaluate *all* the aspects of your attraction—physical, intellectual, emotional, and spiritual—and figure out if your chemistry is real and has the potential to last. And that should be anything but boring.

How would The Wait help you evaluate all aspects of your attraction? Why is that a good idea?

Lord, it is so hard to wait, but I trust that You are using this time to transform me, to make me ready for the person You are bringing to my life. Amen.

....

....

....

....

....

....

....

....

....

....

....

WHO IS YOUR HUSBAND?

Husbands, love your wives, just as Christ loved
the church and gave himself up for her.
—*Ephesians 5:25 NIV*

God's definition of *your* husband is that man who helps you become the best version of yourself and wants you to help him do the same. He's the man who values and respects you for your ownership of yourself. Your husband is the man whose strengths complement your own, who brings out the best of your talents, wisdom, intelligence, and compassion. He's the man who will not diminish you to lift himself up, but rather takes joy and pride in your accomplishments, even if they exceed his own. He's the fully realized man God has meant you to be with.

This man will also respect you in your restraint in practicing The Wait. He's the man who won't run away when you tell him you're abstaining from sex because he understands and appreciates the reasons you're doing it. He might already be on the same path himself. Your husband is the person you were meant to be with, put into your path by God. He's your partner in purpose. He will challenge you in new ways, see things you might have missed, and believe in you when no one else does (sometimes even you).

Which of these characteristics of "your husband" most speaks to you? If you are currently in a relationship, does this man have these qualities?

Lord, I trust You to lead me to the man you have chosen to be my husband. Be with me—and him—while I wait. Amen.

....
....
....
....
....
....
....
....
....
....
....
....
....
....
....
....
....
....

WHO IS YOUR WIFE?

A wife of noble character who can find? She is worth far more than rubies. Her husband has full confidence in her and lacks nothing of value. She brings him good, not harm, all the days of her life.
—*Proverbs 31:10–12 NIV*

Your wife is more than the woman whose finger you put a ring on. She's the perfect fit for your best male qualities, the point to your counterpoint. Your wife is the woman God intends you to be with, and she may be nothing at all like the women you once chased (or still chase) for their looks or the promise of another one-night stand. Your wife is:

- Careful consideration and common sense tempering your bull-facing-the-red-cape impulsivity. She cools you off, calms you down, and helps you see the whole picture before you attack the situation.

- The one who calls out immature man-boy nonsense and reminds you that you're better than that.

- The partner who loves your passionate, change-the-world nature and helps you understand that raw energy, channel it, and use it to create the future.

- Your spiritual guide. Your wife can help you listen to that soft inner voice of the Lord.

- A counterweight to your masculine brute force. She possesses persuasiveness and subtlety. If you can't get what you want through a hostile takeover, what about a handshake?

Once you see that your fear of losing your freedom is an illusion, you'll start to appreciate how finding your wife can enhance not only your spiritual life but also your material life and every measure of personal success.

> Which of these characteristics of "your wife" most speaks to you? If you are currently in a relationship, does this woman have these qualities?

Lord, I trust You to lead me to the woman you have chosen to be my wife. Be with me—and her—while I wait. Amen.

....
....
....
....
....
....
....

ASKING THE RIGHT QUESTIONS

"Ask and it will be given to you; seek and you will find; knock and the door will be opened to you."
—*Matthew 7:7* NIV

One of the challenges—and greatest benefits—of The Wait is staying engaged in getting to know someone you're dating while still remaining objective. Yes, you can still dance and kiss and hold hands and enjoy being together. But part of you should always have your eyes wide open for telltale signs, good and bad, that give you clues into the person's character, personality, and perceptions so you can determine if there is genuine compatibility. Remember, you're shopping, not buying.

If the relationship looks promising, don't be afraid to start asking questions. This is where many relationships fail. Many fear asking questions, worrying, "What if the other person gets upset by the things I want to know?" Someone who gets angry about honest questions may have something to hide. Beware.

It's your responsibility to get clarity on whether or not this person is the right one for you, so keep asking. When we first started dating, our biggest questions were about what we wanted out of life:

- What were our goals?

- Were we at a place where we wanted to get married?

- Where did we see our lives going?

- What was important to us?

Have these conversations early. There's nothing shallow or manipulative about that. If you're not right for each other, it's best to know it immediately. You don't go down that road, falling for that person and wasting your time. You stay on the right road and keep nurturing what matters.

> What are the questions you want answered early on in a relationship? Prepare them now, so you'll be ready.

Lord God, You promise that if I ask, then I will receive. So I am asking You to come alongside me in my dating relationships. Pour your wisdom and guidance into me. Amen.

....

....

....

....

CAN YOU HANDLE THE TRUTH?

"Forget the former things; do not dwell on the past. See, I am doing a new thing! Now it springs up; do you not perceive it? I am making a way in the wilderness and streams in the wasteland."
—Isaiah 43:18–19 NIV

There's a difference between asking genuine, relevant questions and asking questions that are just nosy. Here's what we mean. One of the touchiest subjects in any relationship is the other person's past. We are curious creatures, and we want to know who the other person may have slept with, who he or she has dated, and so on. There is no standard rule about whether it's okay to ask or answer these questions. However, we're in Pandora's-box territory now. Before asking questions about your partner's past, ask yourself:

- Is the information relevant?

- Can I handle the truth?

- Will the information bring us closer together or drive us apart?

We've seen many relationships break up because the individuals didn't stop and think before they began to pry. This was a touchy subject for us as well. Because we both work in the same industry and traditionally have dated within that industry, it was likely that we'd know people we had each dated. So we made an informed, mutual decision: we would share certain, but not all, aspects of our dating past.

To this day we have not discussed every single person we've dated. It isn't relevant. That kind of information can plant seeds of judgment, anger, frustration, and jealousy. Bottom line: we trust each other. If there is something that hasn't yet been shared, we know it will come out if it becomes relevant.

Asking questions when dating is critical, but so is knowing which questions to ask and which ones to let go.

Are there certain parts of your own past that you'd like to keep behind you? What information do you really need about your partner's past?

Holy Lord, help me to see—and to accept—the person I date as he or she is now, just as I want to be seen and accepted for who I am now. Amen.

....

....

....

....

....

DIPPING YOUR TOE INTO THE DATING POOL

How can a young person stay on the path of
purity? By living according to your word.
—Psalm 119:9 NIV

So you've been steering clear of the dating scene for a while. You've spent the time you once dedicated to the pursuit of the opposite sex on examining your mistakes, figuring out what you want, and discovering what you deserve. You've been praying, taking classes, and getting healthy. But now you're ready to jump back in.

Great! Go for it. Here are some tips on how to begin while you also practice The Wait:

- *Keep your focus inward and upward.* This is the time to put "I am" before "I want" and let God show you the worthwhile people you need to meet.

- *Go about dating the same way you'd go about looking for a job.* Get out there, be active, and be consistent. Dating takes practice, and the more you meet new people and practice evaluating them objectively, the better you'll get at it.

- *Don't be afraid to use dating services*. You never know how God might use one of these avenues to help you meet the right person.

- *Be patient*. You might have to spend time with a lot of people before you find one who sees you for who you really are. Be sure you don't change yourself to get someone's approval. That is just not something you can live with long term.

- *Be strong*. You'll be tempted to fall back into old dating habits—obsessing over when he or she will call, one-night stands, committing too fast—but don't. Keep your commitment to The Wait and to yourself.

As you get ready to jump back into the dating pool, what are your biggest concerns? How can you prepare now to handle them?

Lord God, more than anything else, I want to stay on the path You have planned for me. Please bring people into my life who will help me do that. Amen.

....

....

....

DIVING BACK INTO DATING

O people, the LORD has told you what is good, and
this is what he requires of you: to do what is right, to
love mercy, and to walk humbly with your God.
—*Micah 6:8* NLT

Whenever you decide to dive back into dating, that doesn't mean you stop waiting. You're just staying objective, rational, and observant while you're going out with people. Here are some tips for being successful at that:

- *Protect your own time*. Studies have shown that people eat more snacks from a clear jar than they do from an opaque one. Point: we want what we see. Even if you like the other person a lot, make sure you protect your space. Have your own independent life. The balance is healthy, and it'll help you stay objective.

- *Journal your thoughts daily*. Seeing your thoughts about your dating life in writing gives you clarity. Write down your opinions, questions, and concerns every day before you turn in. Reread them in the morning.

- *Pray*. Talk to God daily during The Wait. His voice will remind you just what you're trying to achieve and give you the strength to stick with your plan.

- *Reflect on what you're trying to accomplish*. It's easy to get lost in a new relationship. Remember what The Wait is about: slowing down, learning, discovering the other person, and finding the partner God has in mind for you. Recalling this can recharge your discipline to be patient and stay cool.

If you haven't already, begin a journal of your experiences with The Wait. Be brutally honest—with who you are, where you are in your journey, and the ups and downs of it all.

Lord, as I begin this new kind of dating journey, help me to hear Your voice guiding me—and to listen. Amen.

....

....

....

....

....

....

....

....

LOOKING DEEPER

Do not be bound together with unbelievers; for what
partnership have righteousness and lawlessness, or
what fellowship has light with darkness?
—*2 Corinthians 6:14* NASB

So you've met someone who is smart, deep, and spiritual. You'd like to ask him or her out. Now what?

- *Talk.* Ask the important questions: What do you want out of life? From your partner? What's your relationship with God?
- *Share.* Respect the other person's need to know as much about you as you do about him or her.
- *Use every date as a learning opportunity.* Observe and ask questions. You're learning what you like and don't like in this person.
- *Be honest.* If you're not genuinely interested, don't date someone just for the sake of it.
- *Make sure you're spiritually on the same page.* Someone who doesn't share your values is probably not going to be very compatible in the long term.
- *Make sure the person stimulates you intellectually.* If you can't light your fire with wit, intelligence, and humor, you've got nothing.

- *Don't project what you want onto the other person.* Don't ignore a person's flaws because you're desperate to be in a committed relationship.
- *Look at how your potential partner treats other people.* If the person treats other people badly, that's how he or she will treat you when the infatuation wears off.
- *Make sure the person respects you and values your time.* Being late or constantly texting while you are together could be a sign the person doesn't respect you.
- *Don't hesitate to hit the eject button if things don't feel right.* If something seems off, put things on hold until you feel better about the situation. If you never do, stay away.

You'll notice that in this list, there's nothing about appearance or anything superficial. Why do you think that is? Why is it important to look for someone who has the same values as you? Who respects you and stimulates you intellectually?

Lord, it's so easy to get caught up in the superficial side of a relationship. Help me to look deeper, to see beyond appearances and discover who this person really is. Amen.

....

....

....

AN EXCITING BUT PERILOUS TIME

Be strong in the Lord and in his mighty power. Put
on all of God's armor so that you will be able to
stand firm against all strategies of the devil.
—Ephesians 6:10–11 NLT

So you've been practicing The Wait, and you believe it's finally paid off. You've found someone you think you want to spend your life with—your God-ordained wife or husband. That's exciting. You're talking about getting engaged and getting married, and maybe are even planning the wedding. This is an exciting but potentially perilous time. It can be tempting to surrender any reservations you might have and just roll with it. Don't. This is the most critical part of The Wait, when you can have faith but shouldn't abandon reason. You need both.

It's fun to be starry-eyed and in love. But then you start saying things like, "It's meant to be" and "It doesn't matter; this is true love." You start pretending, glossing over differences, and ignoring things that really matter. That's a danger zone. While it's true that when you find the person God intends for you, it really is meant to be, how can you be sure the person you've committed to is that person without learning more? Wait, and don't turn off your rational mind.

This is the time to learn everything you can about how compatible you two are in every area of your lives. It's the time to bring buried issues into the light so you can discuss, understand, and resolve them.

Why are both faith and reason so important at this time? How can growing closer help you to discover more about your potential partner—both things you want to see and perhaps things you don't?

Holy Father, this is such an exciting time. But in all this rush of emotions, help me not to lose sight of my real goal, of becoming who You want me to be. Amen.

....

....

....

....

....

....

....

....

....

....

....

....

COMMITMENT = MARRIAGE

Let marriage be held in honor among all.
—Hebrews 13:4 ESV

When our relationship began, we weren't looking for another boyfriend-girlfriend thing where we spent years in limbo, not really knowing what was happening. It's normal and healthy not to want to be someone's significant other for another two, three, or four years, because all too often that results in wasted time and a lot of baggage. We had both been there, done that.

In other words, we were ready to become committed. Commitment can have a lot of meanings, but for The Wait it has only one: marriage. Make no mistake: all roads lead to marriage. Practicing The Wait, celibacy, dating— it's all part of a journey intended to lead to marriage to the person God intends you to be with.

We understand that there are a lot of unhealthy views of marriage. In our culture, many people are starting to see marriage as old-fashioned. Young people are less likely to marry, and if they do marry, they're waiting longer. That's smart, because the older you get, the more you learn about yourself and what you want.

On the other hand, plenty of people expect marriage to complete them. They treat it like some magical state that will change them as soon as they say "I do." This actually isn't true. Saying "I do" is the beginning, not the end.

You're saying, "I choose you."

What unhealthy views of marriage do you see in the world around you? What is your view of marriage?

Lord, You created marriage. As I travel this road toward marriage, help me to do so in a way that honors Your creation. Amen.

....
....
....
....
....
....
....
....
....
....
....
....
....
....
....
....

THE WAIT VERSUS WAITING AROUND

*The mind of a person with understanding gets
knowledge; the wise person listens to learn more.*
—*Proverbs 18:15 NCV*

If you love someone but dating exclusively is as far as you're willing to go, what you're saying is, "I think you're right for me, but I'm not sure." That's fine for a while, because we all need time to get to know each other. But when that sort of situation goes on and on for years, one or both partners are dodging true commitment.

Maybe they're comfortable with what they have but fear marriage for reasons of their own. Maybe they're not sure the other person is the One and are afraid to wreck a good thing by being honest. People duck marriage for all sorts of reasons, from not wanting to be tied down to not wanting children.

There's a clear line between The Wait and waiting around. If you're just waiting around, you're doing it out of indecision, fear, or laziness. If you and your partner are communicating, sharing, being honest, exploring new things together, and keeping your objectivity, you shouldn't need more than a year to figure out whether God intended you for each other. If you're stuck in one of those stages for much longer, it's time to start asking why.

When do you believe The Wait crosses over the line into waiting around? Why is waiting around not fair to you or your partner?

Lord, please give me the wisdom to know when The Wait has become just waiting around—and the courage to then make a decision. Amen.

....
....
....
....
....
....
....
....
....
....
....
....
....
....
....
....
....
....

DON'T ASSUME

You shall investigate and search out and inquire thoroughly.
—*Deuteronomy 13:14* NASB

There are those relationships that seem stuck in exclusive dating, but there are also relationships that get stuck even before that point, when neither partner can seem to commit to an exclusive relationship. You have a stalemate, a catch-22 situation where both people are waiting on the other to commit before committing themselves. Sometimes this happens because one or both people have been hurt and are overcautious; other times, it's because of irrational fears about cutting off other options or some such nonsense that translates to "I'm still hoping to meet someone hotter/younger/richer/more compliant than you." In any case, if stalemates don't end quickly, they don't end well. Inevitably, one person gets impatient and moves on.

Like so much else, the solution can be found in communication and faith. If you're dating, you should be communicating. With a few honest, inquisitive conversations, it's really not that hard to figure out if someone you're dating is serious or not. If he or she isn't that person, then the pressure's off! You can keep dating for enjoyment, or you can choose to move on to other people. But don't allow your relationship to be one of assumption:

"I assume she's ready for commitment."

"I assume she wants children."

"I assume he wants to get married someday."

Don't assume. Ask. And if you don't get clear answers, ask again. Assumptions can set you up for massive disappointment.

> Have you made assumptions in past relationships? Or in the relationship you're currently in? What makes assumptions a bad idea?

Dear Lord, give me the courage to ask the tough questions and to seek out the truth—about the person I'm dating and myself. Amen.

....

....

....

....

....

....

....

....

....

....

....

REASONS NOT TO COMMIT

*I am counting on the LORD; yes, I am counting
on him. I have put my hope in his word.*
—Psalm 130:5 NLT

There are plenty of good reasons to just say no to commitment.

1. Sometimes we're just not ready for it emotionally. There's still some work we need to do on ourselves, some personal heavy lifting that demands our focus and sacrifice for a while longer.

2. Reluctance to commit often comes from a deep knowing that it's just not time. And that person you're aching for? If that person is who God has set up for you, he or she will be there when you're ready.

3. Another reason to hesitate is because you realize you've chosen a person because she or he was willing to wait—and not much else. Giving up sex for you is a wonderful thing, but you can't build a relationship on that alone.

4. You shouldn't commit because of pressure or fear that you're falling behind, either. Don't rush into

a commitment because everybody else is doing it. The people who pressure us into marriage are often the same ones who ask, "Why didn't it work out?"

5. You also should never commit because it's what someone else wants. When you make a decision just to please someone else, you will *always* make the wrong decision.

There's no shame in going a distance down the road with someone only to decide that long-term commitment isn't best. It's much better than making a false commitment because you fear being alone or making the other person upset. But end the relationship quickly and honestly. It may be painful, but eventually you'll both realize that it was for the best.

Have you felt pressured to commit before you were ready? How can you best handle that pressure?

Holy Lord, guide me with Your wisdom. Bless me with the perception to know when it's time to make a commitment and when it's time to walk away. Amen.

....

....

LEARNING . . . EVERY DATE, EVERY DAY

This is my prayer for you: that your love will grow more and more; that you will have knowledge and understanding with your love.
—*Philippians 1:9 NCV*

Let's say that things are great and you are both ready to commit for all the right reasons. You'll discover that a committed relationship is a master class on human nature. Spending much of your time with one person and sharing the most intimate details of your lives quickly shatters romantic delusions and childish ideas about love at first sight and happily ever after.

Happily ever after does happen, but not every day . . . or even every hour. There are ups and downs, fights and reconciliations, crises and doubts. The mark of a deep, mature, and unbreakable bond is the ability to weather those storms—to respect, admire, appreciate, and love each other even when you disagree, when you're not at your most attractive, or when your schedules are so busy that intimate time is a distant memory. Your goal is to fall in love not with the body, face, clothes, or title but the person—the spirit—underneath. That's who you'll still love madly in fifty years.

For this reason, learning and communicating assume

their most vital roles in this part of The Wait. Ask yourself "why?" about everything.

Do you ever find yourself afraid to ask "why"? Why is that fear a definite red flag? In what ways is a committed relationship like a master class on human nature?

Lord, bless me with a greater knowledge and understanding of Your love and also the love in my relationship. Amen.

....
....
....
....
....
....
....
....
....
....
....
....
....
....

IT'S AN AUDITION

Love must be sincere. Hate what is evil; cling to
what is good. Be devoted to one another in love.
Honor one another above yourselves.
—Romans 12:9–10 NIV

Dating at any stage—particularly if you're dating some-one exclusively with marriage in mind—is like an audition. After all, this is serious business! We're talking about your potential life partner in all things. At this stage, to wait is to watch out for your interests, becoming as sure as possible that this is the husband or wife God has in mind for you. You'll do that only if you keep your head and look at the things he or she does with a critical eye—without being critical of them, of course.

Remember, what's normal for you is not necessarily normal for your partner. What you regard as a virtue, he or she may see as a flaw. You're going to discover things about this person over time that, no matter how well you thought you knew him or her, will throw you—and vice versa. Now's the time to learn how you'll react to those surprises so that, when they come later, you can respond not with judgment but compassion, clarity, and love.

If you choose to see each date as an audition for marriage, does that change the way you date? Are you, yourself, ready to be auditioned?

Lord God, help me to be sincere in my dating relationship. But even more important, help me to be sincere in my relationship with You. Amen.

....
....
....
....
....
....
....
....
....
....
....
....
....
....
....
....
....
....

PASSION AND CHEMISTRY

Kiss me and kiss me again, for your love is sweeter than wine.
—Song of Solomon 1:2 NLT

Even if you're practicing The Wait and remaining celibate, you still need to assess whether you and the person you're dating have passion chemistry. This is very important. Just because you practice The Wait doesn't guarantee you're going to have a great sex life when you get married.

A great sex life has a lot to do with the chemistry you have with the person you're getting serious with. Is there a passion between you? Desire that goes beyond the strictly physical? How intense does it get when you kiss? It's important to monitor this (obviously within the confines of still practicing The Wait) because it matters. Marriage doesn't automatically light a stove where the pilot light was out. So don't be afraid to kiss each other or hold each other, because if there isn't passion chemistry, this is a red flag that you'll need to address (through counseling, books, or pastoral help) if you want to have a strong and healthy marriage.

How will you walk the line between remaining true to The Wait while determining if your relationship has the passion chemistry it will need in order to succeed?

Holy Lord, You created passion and chemistry, and you intended for that passion to be part of the marriage relationship. Show me how to ensure that passion is present without dishonoring my commitment to You. Amen.

....
....
....
....
....
....
....
....
....
....
....
....
....
....
....
....

THE FRIENDS-AND-FAMILY PLAN

Only simpletons believe everything they're told!
The prudent carefully consider their steps.
—*Proverbs 14:15* NLT

When you get serious about someone, you're excited to tell your friends and family all about it. And they're just as excited, firing endless questions and speculating about marriage, kids, the whole thing. We've both had relationships where our significant others became as intertwined with our families as they did with us. But not knowing how to manage friends and family can make it harder to handle commitment with objectivity and restraint.

Friends and family members tend to fall into two camps: *defenders* and *advocates*. Defenders are skeptical, even cynical, about the person you're dating. Is she good enough for you? Has he unfriended his ex-girlfriends? They're looking out for your interests, and while they can ask some good questions, they can easily cross over into the negative, finding fault where there isn't any.

Advocates are never critical about the person you're with, even when they should be. They're all about the ring and when you'll pop the question. They could push you to move faster than you're comfortable going. Obviously, this is potentially a problem. Being in The Wait is about being patient and letting things develop in their own time.

However, if you manage friends and family right, they can be assets to your journey as a couple. And managing the "help" of family and friends is actually pretty simple. *Wait*. If you don't want them intruding into your dating life, then wait to tell them about the one you like until you're ready to pursue a deeper relationship.

How do your friends and family typically react to potential partners? Do you have advocates, defenders, or some of both? What's your plan to handle them?

Lord, I am so grateful for the friends and family You've placed in my life. But help me to remember that my greatest counsel comes from listening to You. Amen.

....

....

....

....

....

....

....

....

....

....

A WORD ABOUT COUNSELING

Plans fail for lack of counsel, but with many advisers they succeed.
—*Proverbs 15:22 NIV*

About the time it became clear we were on the road to real commitment, we discovered an online assessment specifically designed for couples who are considering getting engaged. We took the results of that and spent the next four months in pre-engagement counseling, discussing everything you can imagine: money, sex, upbringing, spirituality, raising children. We left nothing to chance.

After all, life and marriage throw enough surprises at you, so why leave anything to chance when you're choosing the partner who will be by your side? What's romantic about not fully knowing the person you're marrying?

There are a lot of ways to do this. We highly recommend the kind of in-depth process we went through. Having all those facts on the table and a professional counselor to help us sort through them really put us on a firm footing. But you might also consider:

- *Spiritual counseling.* Talking with your minister or lay spiritual counselor about your beliefs, relationship with God, and other issues can be very revealing.

- *Regular Q&A sessions*. Schedule one night every week or two where you sit down and talk about a specific topic that's relevant to your future: goals, children, lifestyle, parents, mutual interests, and so on.

- *Travel*. Traveling together is the classic test of a relationship's health. You're under stress, sharing common space, often with different expectations.

Find your own way, but find a way. Take your time to figure out if this person really is the one God intends for you to be with.

Would you be willing to do some sort of pre-engagement counseling? How might it be beneficial?

Lord, lead me to those who will give me wise and godly counsel. And help me always to listen to Your perfect counsel. Amen.

....

....

....

....

....

....

LIVING TOGETHER

Give honor to marriage.
—Hebrews 13:4 NLT

Once people think they're with the person God wants them to marry, they often take the next step: move in together. For us, living together wasn't even on the table. We saw that God was setting us up for something incredible, and we wanted to take the time to really get to know each other without the pressure of pretending we were already husband and wife.

It's essential to avoid acting like you're married before you actually are. Because the thing is, you're not married. Cohabitation is another form of limbo where one or both of you can easily start presuming that you should be treated like a spouse even though you're not. Marriage is a formal, powerful commitment: "I choose you and no one else." Until you and your partner have made that commitment, you could still be eyeing the exits when tempers flare, schedules conflict, or a big argument erupts.

Acting married when you're not can set you up for heartbreak. If someone's not committing to you permanently, it's usually for a reason. The person isn't sure. He or she isn't ready. There's nothing wrong with that; however, your potential partner should take the time to get sure and ready! But that may not be as likely to happen if you're living together.

Lots of couples live together thinking it's the logical next step before marriage, but that decision may actually move you further away from getting married. You're already acting like you're married, so why bother with the formality? And that kind of thinking is not what The Wait is about.

> What are your thoughts on living together before marriage? What are God's thoughts?

Lord, You created the commitment of marriage for a reason because it was best for Your people. Help me honor Your creation. Amen.

....

....

....

....

....

....

....

....

....

....

....

LOOKING TOWARD MARRIAGE

*The LORD says, "I will make you wise and show you
where to go. I will guide you and watch over you."*
—*Psalm 32:8 NCV*

Waiting to commit to a relationship until you have
life experience is a smart move. It helps you understand who you want to be. It helps you understand the purpose that God has in mind for you.

For whatever stage of dating and The Wait you're currently in, as you look toward the goal of marriage, here is some other advice we'd like to share with you:

- *Don't base your marriage on preconceived ideals.* Let your marriage find its rhythm. Every marriage is a unique organism; it's important to give that organism time to live, evolve, and settle into what it's going to be.

- *Don't expect your partner to change because you're married.* You can't change someone else in marriage, but marriage will change you.

- *Have a clear sense of your own identity before you marry.* If you don't know who you are before you get married, marriage will not teach you. Instead, you'll become a person's husband or wife and then someone's mom or dad. You'll lose yourself. Understand who you are as a union, but also understand who you are independent of the union.

Whatever road you take, we wish you a marriage that's as joyous and blessed as ours has been.

> Think of a couple whose marriage you admire. What are the traits you admire most? What steps can you take now to ensure that your marriage has those same qualities? If possible, ask that couple about being your marriage mentors.

Holy Lord, I know that marriage is about more than finding the right one; it's also about being the right one. Change me so that I am the right person for my future spouse. Amen.

....

....

....

....

....

....

....

....

....

BUT NOTHING'S HAPPENING

*As for me, I watch in hope for the LORD, I wait
for God my Savior; my God will hear me.*
—Micah 7:7 NIV

If you have been celibate for a time and still have not met your spouse, you may find yourself saying, "I've been waiting but nothing's happening. What now?" The frustration is understandable. First, let's get one thing clear: *The Wait always produces results*. If you have been patiently hoping for better days in your romantic life but aren't seeing them yet, here are some possible reasons why:

- *You're waiting for a certain person*. Do you believe that by your practicing The Wait, God will bring that certain someone into your path? It's possible, but not probable. Don't be so fixated on one person that you pray for him or her instead of God's will.

- *You're waiting for God to do all the work*. You can't just stop having sex, then sit at home and say, "Okay, Lord, I'm ready for you to bring me my spouse!" You have to put in the work to become your best self, and then God will put you into your best life.

- *You don't really know why you're waiting.* Everyone reaches the point of throwing up their hands and swearing off the opposite sex forever. But most of us get our groove back after a weekend of moping and head back out to try again. If you haven't, and you're just on indefinite hold and hoping something good will happen, you're probably going to wind up even more frustrated.

If The Wait doesn't seem to be working, step back and analyze *how* you've been waiting. Because the "how" makes all the difference.

Do you feel like The Wait is working for you? If so, how? If not, ask yourself if maybe it is working—just not in the ways you thought it would.

Lord, help me to remember that even in those times when nothing seems to be happening, You are busy working in my life. Amen.

....
....
....
....
....

FEAR IS A FAILURE OF FAITH

"Fear not, for I have redeemed you;
I have called you by name, you are mine."
—Isaiah 43:1 ESV

I t takes courage and faith to wait for your husband. Because the greatest fear of all is the fear that God will not keep His promises. He won't come through for you.

But God doesn't fail to deliver. It takes guts to face your fears and say, "I have faith that God is going to bring me the right person, so I'm going to wait until He does." If you can find the courage to let a man walk away, you can find the courage to wait.

MEAGAN: There's a belief among some women that if they aren't proactive, they won't end up with anyone. The question is, why do you want to be with someone? If your reason is, "Another man might not come along," you're in a bad place. You're acting purely out of fear, and that means you don't trust God.

This is true for so many things in life. When you frantically chase after something, like a dog chasing a car, it actually becomes harder and harder to catch. You start making compromises and forgetting who you are, and before long you've become someone else. That's true for love, career, wealth, you name it.

But when you focus on doing the right things and becoming a person to whom good things happen, good things do happen. The process of finding your husband isn't really about finding your husband but about finding yourself as a woman.

> How is fear a failure of faith? To combat this fear, read Isaiah 43:1–2. While there have been trials to pass through, how many times has God seen you safely through to the other side?

Lord, I know that in this life there will be waters to walk through and fires to face, but I am so thankful that I never have to walk alone. You are always with me. Amen.

....

....

....

....

....

....

....

....

....

WAITING WITH FAITH

If anyone is in Christ, he is a new creation. The old
has passed away; behold, the new has come.
—*2 Corinthians 5:17* ESV

Faith can pose a problem even for men who have tired of dating multiple women. Many men lack patience. We don't like to wait for things to come to us. We don't wait, period.

But that's a trap. Distractions may reduce the temptation to have sex, but if your focus is not on the patience required to grow your faith, you're not going to do the deep personal work you need to be ready for the woman you're meant to be with. Money, sex, possessions, position, and title distract us from spiritual development. Eventually, you need to stop and go toe to toe with the hard questions:

- What do I want?

- Why am I not happy?

- What is my purpose?

Men often bulldoze through such questions instead of sitting with them, getting to know them. Our culture discourages vulnerability, introspection, and doubt in men.

These qualities are perceived as weakness. But we've been sold an image that's actually damaging men.

Becoming a worthy husband means embracing vulnerability, introspection, and doubt. Men have the potential to be just as healing, noble, nurturing, and high-minded as women if they hold themselves to a higher standard. That doesn't mean becoming less of a man. It means becoming a different kind of man, one who can shed the Neanderthal mentality of his younger years for greater wisdom, restraint, tenderness, and faith. This means finally leaving the adolescent boy behind and embracing the power of real manhood. There's nothing weak or unmanly about that.

Set aside some time today to really wrestle with the questions posed above. Are you willing to shed the stereotype of manliness our culture encourages and embrace the man God created you to be?

Holy Lord, help me to be honest with myself about who I am. And help me to commit to becoming the man You created me to be. Amen.

....

....

....

....

....

PLENTY TO DO WHILE YOU'RE WAITING

Make every effort to give yourself to God as the kind of person he will approve. Be a worker who is not ashamed and who uses the true teaching in the right way.
—*2 Timothy 2:15 NCV*

The Wait is just as much about self-improvement through delayed gratification as it is about love. The clearer you are about how you want to better yourself while you're waiting, the more successful you will be. These are some of the important areas we suggest you focus on if you're planning your own time of waiting:

- Health and fitness
- Personal finance (paying off debts, buying a house, investing for retirement)
- Career
- Education
- Travel
- Entrepreneurship (starting a business, working for a start-up)
- Spirituality (going to church more regularly, honing your openness to the Word, becoming adept at prayer, learning to read God's signs and portents)

- Creativity (painting, acting, composing music, writing a novel, doing stand-up comedy)

- Helping others, doing charitable work, etc.

> Things happen when you have a plan. Pick one (or more) of these areas, and write out a detailed plan for how you will improve yourself in that area. Then get to it.

Lord, I know You have a perfect plan for my life, and I also know that I need to be active in seeking it. Show me the way. Amen.

....
....
....
....
....
....
....
....
....
....
....
....

THE WAIT AND ... WEIGHT

No discipline is enjoyable while it is happening—it's painful! But afterward there will be a peaceful harvest of right living for those who are trained in this way.
—Hebrews 12:11 NLT

When we started talking about the concept of The Wait and the idea of delaying gratification to get what you want, people were most excited about the idea not as it relates to sex but to weight loss. Nothing, not even sex, stands for instant gratification in our culture more than food. For food, you just have to open the fridge!

Delaying gratification to lose weight makes sense. It's a binary situation: either you eat when you're craving food that isn't good for you or you don't. But if you can delay that need for a quick fix, you can see results over time. Since, according to the experts, weight loss is 80 to 90 percent about diet, losing weight really is about controlling what goes in your mouth.

Simple principles can really help: remove temptation (remove from your house those foods that tempt you the most), choose someone you trust to hold and keep you accountable, and work on focusing your attention on the body and health you want more than focusing on the food

you can't eat. And pray for strength every step of the way.
You'll make it.

> Appetites—whether they are for food, for money, or
> for sex—can get us into terrible trouble when left
> uncontrolled. Is there an "appetite" in your life that
> you need to rein in? What steps will you take to
> control it?

*Lord God, You have blessed me so richly. Teach me to enjoy
Your blessings in the right way and at the right time. Amen.*

....

....

....

....

....

....

....

....

....

....

....

....

....

TRUSTING WHAT YOU CAN'T SEE

*Faith is confidence in what we hope for and
assurance about what we do not see.*
—Hebrews 11:1 NIV

The Wait, like any other practice, takes, well, practice. And it has its ups and down. You might start off feeling isolated and sexually frustrated, only to feel the wind at your back as soon as you start a class or talk to your minister. You may go along for months feeling like you're exactly where you need to be, only to run into an old flame and spend the weekend in a depressed funk. The Wait also has its plateaus when it seems like nothing is happening.

Here's the thing: even when it seems like nothing is happening, if you're faithfully doing the work, good things *are* happening. Much of God's work happens behind the scenes. Faith keeps us going through those quiet times, trusting that if we persist, He will reward us.

It's a little like sending a manuscript to a publisher. You do your best work, cast it into the universe, and cross your fingers. Then you wait. The book might sit for months before an editor reads it, but when he does, he loves it and sends you a letter telling you that he wants to publish it. All this time, while your manuscript is waiting to be read and while the congratulatory letter is making its way to your door, you're unaware that something terrific is on its way. Your only recourse is faith. Then one day, the letter arrives and your faith is rewarded.

So keep practicing The Wait . . . good things are coming.

> Have you experienced the ups and downs, the plateaus of The Wait? What keeps you going, faithfully working through The Wait?

Lord, I know and believe that You are working in my life. And I trust that You will reveal Yourself to me when the time is right. Amen.

....
....
....
....
....
....
....
....
....
....
....
....

We do not lose heart. Though outwardly we are wasting
away, yet inwardly we are being renewed day by day.
For our light and momentary troubles are achieving
for us an eternal glory that far outweighs them all.
—2 Corinthians 4:16–17 NIV

So, as far as you know, you've been practicing The Wait just the way we've suggested. You're doing it for the right reasons, doing the work on your mind and character, and staying disciplined about sex. But there's just one problem: nothing has happened, and you're starting to lose hope that it ever will. What are you doing wrong?

First of all, you might not be doing anything wrong. You may just not have practiced The Wait for enough time. The biggest leap of faith lies in not knowing how long it's going to take for your husband or wife to become apparent to you. It could be six months or six years. It will happen when you are mentally, emotionally, and spiritually ready, but there's no way to know when that will be.

There's also no reliable way to speed things up. Seek counseling, go back to church, clean up your diet—those are all beneficial things, but none of them will move up your timetable if God doesn't will it. You don't know when that time is going to come; there could be a crisis on your horizon that will propel you into a new way of thinking. Maybe someone new, who's not your husband or wife, will come into your life to be the bridge to the person who is.

It's difficult for us to say, "Just keep waiting," but that's what we have to do. You must have faith that God will make your wait worthwhile.

What can you do while you "just keep waiting"? What will make your wait worthwhile?

Lord, Your timing is perfect. And one day, all these struggles will seem "light and momentary." Help me to remain faithful until then. Amen.

....
....
....
....
....
....
....
....
....
....
....

DON'T SABOTAGE YOURSELF

*And I am certain that God, who began the good work
within you, will continue his work until it is finally
finished on the day when Christ Jesus returns.*
—*Philippians 1:6* NLT

You've been practicing The Wait for a while now.
You've done your best and you've done it for all the
right reasons. But still . . . no husband, no wife. Just long,
lonely nights with no sex. You may start to ask yourself
why. Why are you practicing The Wait when it doesn't
seem to be bringing you any results?

Don't give up! God *is* working on your behalf, even if
you don't see it right now. What if that meeting with your
future spouse is right around the corner, but you sabotage
it by giving up and going to back to your old ways? That
would be tragic.

Second, we would challenge you to look beyond the
obvious result of finding a marriage partner to some less
obvious—but arguably even more important—benefits of
practicing The Wait. For example, during your wait
have you:

- Experienced less drama and more stable friend-
  ships?

- Dated some really interesting people?

- Gotten to know yourself at a deeper level?

- Let go of past emotional baggage?

- Broken self-destructive behavior patterns?

- Gotten physically fit and mentally healthier?

- Advanced your career?

- Pursued your dreams?

- Become more deeply spiritual and drawn closer to God?

If the answer to any of these questions is yes, you've profited from The Wait. Yes, The Wait is about finding the person God wants you to do great things with, but its core is about personal evolution. It's about being at peace with who you were, who you are, and who you're becoming.

Have you seen benefits in your life from your practice of The Wait? What are they? How can you bring more of those benefits into your life?

Lord, You have begun a good work in me, and I know that You will finish it—in Your own time and in Your own way. I trust in You. Amen.

....

....

WHEN THE WAIT ISN'T WORKING

*Trust in the LORD with all your heart, and do not lean on
your own understanding. In all your ways acknowledge
him, and he will make straight your paths.*
—*Proverbs 3:5–6* ESV

One reason that you might not have found your spouse
is that, to be perfectly honest, you already did. But
you didn't recognize the person as your spouse when he or
she was in front of you, and the opportunity passed you by.
Don't panic. It isn't the end of the world. There are several possibilities at work. You may not have been at a place
in your development where you could "see" that person as
special. Maybe he or she didn't conform to your List, and
you said, "Pass."

If that happened, don't lose hope. The two of us orbited each other for four years before we finally started
dating. If God means for you to be with someone, He will
bring you together.

Another possibility is that you became a different person through your practice of The Wait, and God decided
that the person He originally had in mind for you was not
your ideal partner after all. In that case, your continued
wait may just be a matter of God aligning your path with

the new man or woman who will help you become the best version of yourself.

Whatever the reason you're still waiting, the important thing to remember is The Wait always works—in one way or another. Keep practicing, keep working on being the best you that you can be, and keep intentionally seeking God. He will bring you to where He wants you to be . . . and the person He wants you to be with.

So much of The Wait is trusting God's plan for your life. Does that trust come easily for you? What helps you to keep following The Wait, even when you don't see how God is working?

Holy Lord, teach me to trust You and Your perfect plan, rather than my own understanding. Amen.

....

....

....

....

....

....

....

....

....

STUCK IN A RUT

*Don't you realize that in a race everyone runs, but
only one person gets the prize? So run to win!*
—*1 Corinthians 9:24* NLT

Despite starting The Wait with the best of intentions, it's possible to fall into a rut. Perhaps you stop pushing yourself to grow and learn like you used to, and this has slowed your progress to a crawl. This is more common with long wait periods, because boredom and complacency naturally set in. If you're not seeing electric results from your dating and you've reached your immediate personal goals, it's easy to get too comfortable. Before you know it—*clunk*—you've fallen into a rut that's not much more effective than your previous pattern of behavior.

Some people think the best defense against this sort of thing is discipline, but that will take you only so far. Discipline is good, but we think it's better to have people in your life who will hold you accountable. We do that for each other. Friends, family members, your minister, mentors—any of them can be your accountability check-ins. Tell them about The Wait, what you're doing and why, and what your goal is. Ask them to say something if they see you getting too comfortable or not moving forward in your life.

The Wait is not a checklist—do this, do that, and *BOOM!* results. Instead, it's a process, one that requires constant evaluation and adjustment. But it's a process that will lead you to becoming the person God created you to be.

> Do you have people in your life who will hold you accountable? People who are willing to say the hard things that need to be said? Are you that person for someone else?

Lord, please bring people into my life who will not only encourage me in this time of waiting, but also lovingly and truthfully correct me. Amen.

....

....

....

....

....

....

....

....

....

....

....

....

....

DROP THE BAGGAGE

Forgetting the past and looking forward to what lies ahead, I press on to reach the end of the race and receive the heavenly prize for which God, through Christ Jesus, is calling us.
—Philippians 3:13–14 NLT

If you're still carrying the same baggage that led to your previously dysfunctional romantic life, then you'll find that The Wait probably isn't yielding results for you. Practicing The Wait involves letting go of the old fears, insecurities, and addictive behaviors that messed you up in the past and cleaning up your emotional self. That battered old baggage—feelings of being unloved by your parents, fears lingering in the wake of an abusive relationship, body issues, and so on—drives your behavior. That's why unhealthy relationships tends to follow unhealthy relationships, over and over, until the similarities become almost eerie.

Talk with someone who can help you figure out what baggage you're clinging to, where it comes from, and how to let it go. This can happen quickly, but the length of time doesn't really matter. What matters is getting a spring cleaning of your spirit that lets you go into the world clear-eyed and ready to approach dating and relationships in a new, healthy way.

Because until you can drop that baggage, your relationship patterns aren't likely to change and you probably won't get the results you're hoping for from The Wait.

What relationship baggage are you still carrying? What do you need to do to put it down? Do you just need to let it go, do you need to forgive or confront someone, or do you need to talk to a counselor or minister? Take a positive step today toward putting down your baggage.

Lord, help me to put the mistakes and sorrows of the past behind me and to look forward to the future You have in store for me. Amen.

....
....
....
....
....
....
....
....
....
....
....
....

FINE-TUNING THE WAIT

Encourage each other and give each other strength.
—*1 Thessalonians 5:11 NCV*

I f you've been practicing The Wait, and it's going pretty well, here are some fine-tuning tips that could make it even better.

- *Check in regularly with your accountability partners.* All you really need is a small group of people who care about your well-being. (If they're also practicing The Wait, that's even better!) Meet with them regularly and follow these ground rules: total honesty, constructive criticism, and no judgment.

- *Set clear goals and time frames.* Set specific goals for yourself, such as a certain salary or a target weight. Lay down equally specific schedules. You might not know when your ideal mate is coming, but you can control the rest of the process.

- *Celebrate.* The Wait should be a joyful daily discovery of what you're really capable of. So when you reach a milestone, reward yourself!

- *Pray.* God is at the core of The Wait. Check in with Him often. We suggest a daily prayer, asking for strength and discipline. The Lord will reveal wonders to you if you're quiet and listen to His voice.

- *Keep a journal so you can see how far you've come.* Journaling lets you track where you were and where you are now. When you feel tired or discouraged, go back and read your journal entries. You'll see how far you have come.

- *Heal the past.* You've got to let the past go and move on. That often means confronting and forgiving people who've hurt you. By doing so, you take back your power by taking the high ground—God's ground.

Make praying for God to strengthen you through The Wait a part of your daily routine. And be sure to spend time just listening, as well. Begin by writing out a prayer to Him.

Lord, teach me to recognize Your voice and to listen when You speak. Amen.

THE WAIT AND ... SELF-ESTEEM

See what great love the Father has lavished on us, that we should be called children of God! And that is what we are! The reason the world does not know us is that it did not know him.
—*1 John 3:1 NIV*

Self-esteem is the eight-hundred-pound gorilla in the room, the reason so many of us go astray before discovering The Wait. God may love us, we know, but we don't always love ourselves very much. So many of the problems that we bring upon ourselves, from addiction to remaining in damaging and even abusive relationships, stem from the deep-down belief that we can't do better, don't deserve better.

The Wait comes into play here because rather than confront the reasons we harbor such feelings of worthlessness and self-hatred, we often run from them by pursuing instant gratification. Serial dating, casual sex, drinking, getting wrapped up in other people's dramas—they're often ways to avoid dealing with our own pain. But pain doesn't just heal without attention. It waits beneath the surface and poisons everything in our lives.

The solution is to reject the quick fix of a drink or a one-nighter that temporarily dulls the pain. Face the reasons that you're in pain. It's hard and it's something you shouldn't do alone, but it's definitely something you should do. There is life on the other side of trauma, self-loathing, and bitterness, and it can be amazing. The first step is being willing to stare down your pain and not look away. Do that and you can do the rest.

> Read 1 John 3:1. Do you see yourself as a lavishly loved child of God? Do you expect people to treat you as a lavishly loved child of God? If not, why not? Seek out a trusted friend or counselor, and ask that person to help you sift through how you feel about yourself.

Lord, teach me to better love You and myself, so that I may better love others. Amen.

....
....
....
....
....
....
....
....
....
....
....

GOD IS ... ROMANTIC

There are three things that are too hard for me, really four
I don't understand: the way an eagle flies in the sky, the
way a snake slides over a rock, the way a ship sails on the
sea, and the way a man and a woman fall in love.
—*Proverbs 30:18–19* NCV

Neither of us was perfect in the way that we waited. We both made mistakes. We both questioned what God was doing and resisted His will. We became discouraged and confused. We're far from perfect. The one thing we did that allowed us to date, fall in love, marry, and come to you with this gift was to put our total faith in God. He threw us some surprises and challenges, but we never wavered in our belief that He was building a foundation under us that would lead us to glory. The experience of our romance has taught us so much, but this is one of the most surprising things we've learned:

God is romantic.

Admittedly, that's probably not the first word that comes to mind when you think of the Lord. *Demanding*, sure. *Benevolent*, absolutely. But *romantic*? Think about it. What's more romantic than knowing that there is a perfect person (truly, more than one) for you out there in the world and that he or she is slowly walking his or her winding path toward the place and time when you will meet? You don't know when you'll cross paths or how. You don't know if you'll instantly be attracted or just be friends for a while. All you know is that there is a love of your life who will one day be yours when you're ready. God's directing a really great script . . . for you.

Have you ever thought of God as romantic? Take some time to read Song of Songs. Does it surprise you that God's view of the marriage relationship is a decidedly romantic—and sexual—one?

Lord God, open my eyes to see this romantic side of You and all the ways it plays out in my life and in this world. Amen.

GREAT THINGS ARE COMING

"No eye has seen, no ear has heard, and no mind has imagined what God has prepared for those who love him."
—*1 Corinthians 2:9 NLT*

Wherever you are in your journey to find the love of your life, our best advice is to trust God and have faith. You can trust God to do right by you if you do right by Him—entering The Wait honestly, with good intentions, and doing your best to honor your commitment. Just don't give up. And if you fall, don't dwell on it. Dust yourself off. Ask for forgiveness and get right back to your commitment. Sometimes, God doesn't bring people into our lives in the way we expect or in the time we expect, but that doesn't mean He's not working in your life to make wonderful things happen. It just means that you have to have faith.

Great things are coming. Better yet, great things are already here! Even if love isn't on your doorstep at this very moment, with every day that passes, you're becoming wiser, stronger, and more in control of who you're becoming. That's amazing. Believe in God just as He believes in you. Keep your focus, take a deep breath, and don't give up on The Wait. Let God work on you and within you. Right now—today—is the beginning of the relationship, and the life, that you've always dreamed of and the one you've been praying for.

> Take some time to think about where you started and where you are now in this journey. Are your current strategies working? Do you need to make some adjustments?

Lord, throughout this whole process of The Wait, my greatest desire has been to draw closer to You. Thank You for always walking right beside me. Amen.

....
....
....
....
....
....
....
....
....
....
....
....
....
....
....

JOURNAL PAGES

JOURNAL PAGES

JOURNAL PAGES

JOURNAL PAGES

JOURNAL PAGES

JOURNAL PAGES

JOURNAL PAGES

JOURNAL PAGES

JOURNAL PAGES

JOURNAL PAGES

JOURNAL PAGES

JOURNAL PAGES

ABOUT THE AUTHORS

DeVON FRANKLIN is a spiritual success coach and the CEO of Franklin Entertainment, a production company in conjunction with 20th Century Fox. He is the producer of the box office hit *Miracles from Heaven* and the animated film *The Star.* He hosted the hit TLC event series *This Is Life Live.* Beliefnet called him one of the "Most Influential Christians Under 40." He is the author of the *New York Times* bestseller *The Wait, Produced by Faith,* and *The Hollywood Commandments.* He graduated from the University of Southern California.

MEAGAN GOOD is an award-winning actress, bestselling author, and producer. She has toplined some of Hollywood's biggest blockbusters, including *Think Like a Man, Think Like a Man Too, Anchorman 2: The Legend Continues, Stomp the Yard*, and the critically acclaimed *Eve's Bayou.* She also starred in *Deception* for NBC and *Minority Report* for Fox. She is the *New York Times* bestselling author of *The Wait.* She's the cofounder of The Greater Good Foundation, a nonprofit organization that advocates for the empowerment and enrichment of young women.

DeVon and Meagan married in the summer of 2012 and live in Los Angeles.